FINANCIAL ABUSE OF THE ELDERLY:

A Detective's Case Files Of Exploitation Crimes

Publisher: Ruby House Pub
Rights Owner: Joseph Roubicek

ISBN: 978-0-6151-8514-9

~ INTRODUCTION ~

While the number of violent crimes in the U.S. is decreasing, financial crimes against the elderly are increasing as a result of the aging of the population and greater concentration of wealth among older people. According to a 2005 Senior Forum Report by the White House Conference On Aging, only one in 100 cases of financial abuse is reported, and there are millions of financial abuse victims each year. The money is certainly there for the taking: persons over 50 control at least 70% of the nation's household net worth. 75% of victims of financial abuse are between the ages of 70 and 89. The majority are female, frail and mentally impaired.

The Senior Forum Report pointed to a lack of knowledge regarding scams and the inability of seniors to recognize scams and make sure their financial matters are in order. But victims who are "frail and mentally impaired" simply cannot protect themselves. It is up to the rest of us—family members, neighbors, friends, and those of us who come into contact with the elderly in our work, whether as bank tellers, attorneys, health care professionals, or service providers of any kind, to help them protect themselves. Armed with knowledge, we can take steps in advance to prevent ourselves from becoming victims when we become old and infirm.

Fraud Vs. Exploitation

Since 1990 I have investigated more than 1,000 cases of exploitation of the elderly during my former career as a detective with the Fort Lauderdale Police Department. During this time I've realized that reports that address financial crimes against the elderly usually conflate two types of crimes, fraud and exploitation. Fraud is based on deception, but exploitation of the elderly is a much subtler and much more often ignored crime. Justice Potter Stewart's famous definition of pornography applies equally to exploitation crimes: I may not be able to define it precisely but I know it when I see it.

Definitions of fraud found in dictionaries, or state and federal laws, are essentially based on deception. When referring to the theft of physical property, fraud is basically defined as the false and deceptive statement of fact intended to induce another person to give up a valuable item he or she owns. Scams, confidence games, rackets, hoaxes and shakedowns are common terms used to describe misrepresentations and trickery used by con men or women to entice their target into making bad decisions.

"Choice" is involved with fraud and there is an assumption in state laws throughout the nation that fraud victims have the capacity to weigh information and make decisions based on that information. But what if the victim does not have capacity?

That's when the crime may actually be exploitation rather than fraud. The dictionary defines exploitation as selfish or unfair use of someone or something for one's own advantage, taking advantage of another person in an organized or systematic way. My own state, Florida, defines an exploitation victim as "a person 60 years of age or older who is suffering from the infirmities of aging as manifested by advanced age or organic brain damage, or other physical, mental, or emotional dysfunctioning, to the extent that the ability of the person to provide adequately for the person's own care or protection is impaired." An exploitation crime occurs when someone takes advantage of the vulnerability or dependant condition of a disabled elderly person to deprive that person of their assets. So while elderly fraud victims are independent persons with the capacity to give consent, exploitation victims are disabled in some manner and this disability contributes to their victimization.

Exploitation victims came from all walks of life and every socioeconomic group. The perpetrators often turned out to be those we would least expect: neighbors, spiritual leaders, nurses, guardians, even the mailman or plumber on occasion.

I have written this book by drawing on my first-hand experience that presents a group of interesting cases that illustrate the nature of exploitation crimes. These cases are "the real thing," based on facts. I explain how to recognize and prevent victimization through better understanding and by implementing simple safeguards. Each chapter presents a case from my files that provide analysis of why the elderly person was victimized.

Exploiters are usually very successful criminals and crimes that succeed soon become epidemic. My goal here is simple. I want independent senior citizens to protect themselves, and the average "Joe" to be able to protect an older loved one. One day we will all be in the same boat and by taking action now we protect ourselves for the future.

FINANCIAL ABUSE OF THE ELDERLY;
A Detective's Case Files Of Exploitation Crimes

By Joe Roubicek

TABLE OF CONTENTS

CHAPTER I

CONMEN AND DRIFTERS

9:30 AM, February 10TH 1990

"Make a right here! Go right!" I yelled at my partner.

We turned with tires screeching onto 10th Terrace from Southeast 15th Street in our unmarked police car. The white van we were chasing had just turned right, a block ahead, and I hoped we could beat it to Southeast 17th Street to cut it off.

I keyed my radio, "Kilo 48, we're southbound approaching 17th Street now."

A two man patrol unit stepped in. "Bravo 301, we're a block away on 17th Street, standing by. We'll pick it up here. What's the reference?"

"Gypsies, home improvement fraud, white Ford van, unknown tag, occupied by at least two white males."

Bravo 301 took over the chase on 17th Street and we sped southbound on Federal Highway towards the international airport.

Morning rush-hour was still winding down and traffic was heavy enough to keep the van from getting very far away from us, but the driver pulled a quick U-turn onto the grassy median between the northbound and southbound lanes. A good escape tactic, if not for the drainage ditch running along the center of the median. Their vehicle swung around, wheels spinning into the earth, as it fishtailed northbound.

Bravo 301 couldn't react in time and continued south, but we stayed on the van, swinging our car north and following the vehicle right into the drainage ditch. The driver of the van struggled with the steering wheel but lost control. The van flipped onto its right side and slid about 30 yards along the ditch, papers flying out its windows, before finally coming to a rest. Our car was right behind it, thankfully still upright. But now our brakes locked and the car skidded dangerously.

Things seemed to be moving in slow motion, which isn't good because that usually means an accident is happening. But we stopped just short of a collision, our bumper coming right up to the van's exposed undercarriage.

The van's driver and passenger crawled out of the driver-side window almost as quickly as my partner, Bud, and I exited our car. But by now the two men had had enough and quickly spread-eagled on the ground after seeing our drawn guns.

It was a messy scene in the median: two cars in a trench, a van on its side with paperwork scattered about. The papers were contracts – dozens of home improvement deals signed by unwitting elderly victims throughout South Florida.

Winter in Fort Lauderdale: the tourist season. Along with the tourists come various groups of con artists. It's an annual event in South Florida. Groups broadly labeled by politically incorrect law enforcement authorities as the "Irish Gypsies" were well known for conducting various forms of home improvement fraud. These con artists preyed on the elderly, often collecting thousands of dollars from a single victim for unneeded repairs.

I received this complaint less than two hours before the chase occurred. The nephew of an elderly woman had discovered that she had written a $5,000 check for roof repairs. He also found a $5,000 contract that she had signed to have leaks fixed, though the roof was in excellent condition. While he was questioning his aunt, the phone rang. After a short conversation, she hung up and told her nephew that the "repair man" said he lost the first check and was returning to get another. The nephew promptly called the Fort Lauderdale Police Department and within a half-hour Bud and I were parked two houses away from the victim's home. We were sitting in an unmarked police car, waiting for the suspects' return.

When they did come back, my partner and I stepped out of our vehicle and approached theirs. The two men were not happy to see the police. They fled in a desperate effort to escape, leading us on our chase through city streets.

Now that the chase had ended, the officers of Bravo 301 drove the suspects away for booking. I returned to the victim's home to take her statement.

She was a very pleasant, frail woman in her 80s and when I sat down with her, I expected the statement to be routine. But when I asked her to give an account of what happened, she hesitated and meekly admitted not remembering much of anything. I showed her the $5,000 contract that she signed for her roof repairs and again she had no memory of signing it. She said that if the men told her the roof leaked, then it was probably true. She was actually concerned that she might be in trouble.

After I assured her that she was not the person who had done anything wrong, she refused to prosecute the men. I began to feel silly for even asking her to press charges because from her point of view she was not a victim.

When I left the poor lady's house, both of us felt miserable. She couldn't remember what happened and didn't know what to do about it. She felt anxious, guilt-ridden and confused. On the other hand, I knew what happened. I had arrested the bad guys but had a victim who didn't want to prosecute.

Walking to our car I said to Bud, "Well, that went well!"

Bud laughed. "Right. Glad it's your case! And keep my name out of the report. I don't want to go to court on this one," he said.

By coincidence, or perhaps destiny, I worked on a similar case that same week involving a 79-year-old woman. She had been befriended by a drifter who took her life savings of $1,200. Not much, but all that she had. Like my first victim, her short-term memory was severely impaired.

His name was David Bostic, a 26-year-old ex-convict with a prior conviction for every color in the crayon box. His scheme was simple. He just filled out the woman's checks, asked her to sign them, then drove her to the bank each day to cash them. He waited in the lobby, which was monitored by the bank's cameras, where he took the money from her.

After some anxious research through the state statute books, I was able to find a law that was almost never used in the state of Florida at that time –"Financial Exploitation of an Elderly or Disabled Person." It recognized the vulnerable elderly population that suffered disabilities and had also just been increased from a misdemeanor to felony status. The law was written to protect disabled persons of all ages, but it specifically recognized the elderly population because the aging process *is* a disabling process.

Put simply, the law states that when an elderly person suffers physical or mental disabilities and a person takes advantage of these disabilities to steal the elderly person's assets, this is financial exploitation. Most states have an exploitation law similar to Florida's.

Armed with this new weapon, I made sure that Bostic and the two home-improvement con men were all charged that same week.

These exploitation arrests were among the very few made in the state and that caught the media's eye, but while the media sensationalized the "con" or deception in these crimes I knew that this wasn't really the issue. With each new case I realized that the key is not deception of the elderly, but exploitation of common disabilities this population suffers. Exploiters were being recognized as crafty scammers when they were simply exploiting the victim's disabilities.

I had no idea at the time that my law enforcement career was about to focus on a billion dollar crime that would devastate so many.

CHAPTER 2

GOVERNMENT GOOF-UPS

April 1990

Greta was 95-years-old and her health was pretty good for a "near-centenarian." She had just set the pen down after signing a very important document for her new caretaker, Veleta Cossie, and it went as follows:

Date: 4-12-90

To Whom It May Concern

This is to certify that I, Greta H. Crowley, relinquish all my shares and interest in all the various companies:

(1)   Texas Utilities Company

(2)   General Electric Company

(3)   General Motors Company

(4)   CommonWealth Edison Company

(5)   G.M. Hughes Electric Company

To Veleta Cossie for her kindness shown to me.

Sincerely Yours,

Greta Crowley

Veleta Cossie read over the $125,000 gift letter carefully before putting it in a safe place. She was concerned about being accused of stealing from the elderly woman, but you can't have a crime without a victim. And Greta had signed the gift letter voluntarily.

On June 27, two months later, I was sitting with Greta Crowley in her home, taking her taped statement as a different caretaker sat by her side. The tape recorder was on a coffee table between us. I pushed the record button and spoke:

(Taken from actual statement transcript.)

"The following is the statement of Greta Crowley. This statement is being taken on June 27th, 1990 at 2606 Del Mar Place, Fort Lauderdale, commencing at 1:25 P.M. Greta, could you tell me what your date of birth is?"

"August 10th."

"What year?"

"I don't know."

"Do you know what day today is?"

"No."

"Today is Wednesday, Greta. Do you remember Veleta, the nurse's aide that took care of you a while back?"

"No, I really don't especially."

"Do you remember giving this gift letter, your stocks, or anything to Veleta?"

"No. You told me her name, but if she walked in the door I wouldn't know her."

"Could you tell me what your address here is, Greta?"

"406 Del Mar Island."

"406 Del Mar Island?"

"Is that right? Is that here? 406 Del Mar?"

Greta was in good physical health for a 95-year-old, but she suffered acute short-term-memory loss. I had received a call the prior day from a local bank representative, who was alerted to the gift letter a broker was using to transfer ownership of the stocks over to Cossie's name.

Back in February, about the same time we chased that white van through the neighborhood, Greta Crowley was already being exploited -- not by Cossie but by a woman who presented herself as Greta's niece. This suspect fled when the state Adult Protective Services (APS) responded to an anonymous complaint. Department investigators had determined that Greta no longer possessed the capacity to make financial decisions or care for herself. An emergency guardianship hearing was requested.

A local bank was assigned as the guardian of her assets and a placement agency, Atlas Guardianship Services, was made the guardian of her "person." Atlas Guardianship Services assigned one of their employees, Veleta Cossie, to Crowley's home.

In only two weeks, Cossie had Greta signing the gift letter.

The courts had selected Atlas from a list of agencies that had not been checked for licensing and the agency was not properly licensed.

Atlas was supposed to check for criminal backgrounds of all employees, but they never checked the background of Veleta Cossie. If they had, they would have found that she had been arrested two years prior for attempted murder after beating another woman over the head with a lead pipe. In a plea bargain, Cossie had plead guilty to aggravated battery and the judge had withheld adjudication.

When the investigation was completed, I finally located Cossie providing care in the home of another elderly woman and, though she tried to escape out the back door, she was taken into custody. She claimed that the stocks were a gift and insisted on her innocence.

The media took notice when Cossie went before a magistrate judge the following morning and when a local news reporter interviewed me, I warned that people cannot depend on the government for protection from this crime.

The problems that contributed to Greta Crowley's continued victimization were caused by loose government regulations and just plain negligence. The victim did not have the ability to protect or care for herself, so the government stepped in to protect her, but placed her under the care of a violent thief. They put the proverbial "fox in the henhouse."

But even if the government had taken proper action so that Greta was not exploited a second time, how could they have prevented the first incident? Many exploitation victims are truly "silent victims" because they are typically not aware of their predicament due to mental infirmities. It is not reasonable to expect the government to prevent exploitation crimes that are not reported, just as it is not reasonable to expect the elderly who are mentally disabled to protect themselves. For this reason a person should take action to protect their assets beforehand while they are still able.

CHAPTER 3

"SALT OF THE EARTH"

June, 1990

It was an old and quaint one-story house at 1535 North Atlantic Boulevard, prime property tucked behind a row of palm trees and ficus hedges that ran along the main road, or "strip," bordering the Atlantic Ocean. The salt air had taken its toll on the house and a paint job was sorely needed. A worn-out welcome mat adorned with flying mallards and two words, *The Brewers,* lay by the front door but few visitors had crossed it lately.

Sam and Hildegard Brewer had lived there for decades and with in-home health care they were able to continue to do so despite their disabilities. Sam was an 83-year-old retired Army colonel who had owned a boys' military academy and now was confined to a wheelchair. His 85-year-old wife, Hildegard, was a painter who had inherited most of her family's wealth and was bedridden these days, blinded by macular degeneration. The family doctor had not been to the house in a month and Hildegard had bedsores and weighed less than 90 pounds. Her health had continued to deteriorate despite the caretaker's sincere efforts to help her. Indeed, her only real friend and companion was the caretaker, Marcia Cambell.

Marcia took very good care of both of the Brewers and she was especially close to Hildegard, who considered her to be a trusted and dearly loved friend. Now, though, they were being forced to part company. Marcia sat by Hildegard's bedside, holding her fragile hands while both of them cried and said their farewells. Then Hildegard gently pulled Marcia closer and whispered in her ear, "*Tell the police what's happening here.*"

Hildegard was referring to the actions of another woman, the person she believed was holding her a virtual captive -- Marcia's boss, Trudi Gramazio.

Gramazio was in the family room with Sam at that very moment, explaining that Marcia had been fired because of her unsatisfactory job performance. But in the bedroom, Marcia had just explained to Hildegard that her job had ended for another reason: Gramazio had asked her to intercept the Brewers' mail before Sam could see it. Marcia had refused.

For the past year, Gramazio had nurtured her relationship with Sam Brewer, going from "healthcare provider" to an almost "companion-guardian" status. She became Sam's confidant and financial advisor. She had worked her way into his affections with hugs and kisses of endearment as Marcia watched discreetly and Hildegard listened helplessly from her bed.

Gramazio's name now was attached in some manner to every asset the Brewers owned and the only real obstacle was Marcia. The convenient thing to do was remove Marcia from the scene. So the honest caretaker was forced out and her replacement soon arrived.

But Gramazio had underestimated Hildegard. This deceptive companion never imagined that, in her deteriorated condition, the old woman could give such a competent and valuable statement to the police.

It was the first week of July 1990. I was finishing up the final report on the Greta Crowley case for the prosecutor's office when a phone call from Marcia was transferred to me by the police communications center. Although she was hesitant at first, Marcia expressed her concerns for the welfare and safety of the Brewers and their assets under the care of her former boss, Trudi Gramazio. The one sentence that really stuck out in my mind was Hildegard's comment to her to, "Tell the police what's happening here." That was my motivation to stop by the Brewers that same day to make sure that neither was in immediate danger.

I was in luck because Gramazio was not around and the new caretaker, a small Jamaican woman, allowed me in without question after seeing my badge. My intent was not only to check on the validity of Marcia's complaint but also to get an idea of the mental capacity of the Brewers.

The house was worth about $250,000 at that time and would be valued at well over a million dollars by today's standards. It was in good condition, clean and in order, and at first glance the Brewers seemed to be getting satisfactory care.

There was a large portrait on the family room wall of Sam and Hildegard in their younger days. He wore an Army officer's formal military dress uniform and she was dressed in a beautiful gown, holding his hand and standing proudly by his side. Hildegard's signature was on the lower right corner of the painting.

Now, though, Sam was in his wheelchair just beneath the painting, dozing with his head slumped. There was a stark contrast between this old man and the strong, proud man in the painting.

The caretaker awoke Sam with some significant shouting and then explained to me that his hearing aid had not been working properly for the past couple of weeks. I introduced myself to him and said a complaint had been lodged with the police: We had been told someone might be taking his assets. Then I asked him specifically about his assets to see if he was able to understand the extent of them but he couldn't. Sam could only make general statements such as, "I'm sure there is sufficient money in the bank."

I asked about his relationship and agreements with Gramazio. He said that he trusted her completely and gave her permission to manage his finances because he could no longer do it himself.

While speaking with Sam, I heard the caretaker on the kitchen phone telling someone about my presence. I assumed that it was Gramazio. Because I wasn't quite ready to meet her and needed time to interview the victims, I said goodbye to Sam and headed into Hildegard's bedroom.

In that room was this remarkably tiny, frail old woman lying on her back, staring blankly at the ceiling. As soon as I greeted her, she screamed wildly, seemingly without end. It sounded like someone was hurting her badly and I stepped out of that room in seconds.

The caretaker laughed, saying that Hildegard didn't like strangers much lately. She also said that Gramazio was on her way to speak with me, so using a court appearance as an excuse, I apologized and headed for the door. I left my card and a message for Gramazio: I would be getting in touch with her shortly.

On the way out I saw a small pile of mail on the kitchen counter and noticed a statement from a local bank. I assumed it was for the Brewers and planned on getting a subpoena the next morning to examine their bank accounts.

The couple still had about $40,000 in their checking account. Within the past year, Gramazio's name had been added to that account. More than $70,000 already had passed through the checking account to Gramazio for various home health care expenses and to pay Gramazio's personal bills, such as the veterinarian who cared for her daughter's puppy. Before this, the Brewers had paid for the purchase of the puppy.

In addition to the $70,000, other checks were made out directly to Gramazio for significant amounts, $20,000, $11,000 and $5,000. Her name also had been added to the Brewers' $100,000 certificate of deposit, a quit claim deed for the Brewers' $250,000 property and a new will, which made Gramazio the executor and beneficiary of the Brewers' estate after all debts were paid. To this day, I cannot think of any asset that belonged to the Brewers that was not also the property, or future property, of Gramazio.

Marcia had told me that she heard Gramazio borrow $20,000 from Sam so that she could buy "Extended Nursing Services" from the owner. As a result, I called that business the next morning to speak with the listed owner, Gertrude Berglin. Berglin did answer the phone and after a short discussion, told me that she was also Trudi Gramazio. "Berglin", she explained, was her maiden name and "Trudi" was short for "Gertrude".

Whether I liked it or not, it appeared that I made first contact with Trudi, or Gertrude, or whoever-the-hell she was, and I invited her in to the police department that afternoon for an interview.

Now, more than ever, I wanted to get a taped statement from Sam while the opportunity was there so I quickly returned to the Brewers' residence. Sam was more than happy to give a statement and he appeared to enjoy the attention.

"Do you swear that the statement you're about to make is the truth, the whole truth and nothing but the truth, so help you God?"

"I will, I do."

"Sam, is your wife Hildegard competent? Is she aware of what's going on in her environment?"

"Well, she's aware to a certain degree. Sometimes she hallucinates but other than that, I see no difficulty."

"Okay. Is she aware that your will gives your estate to Trudi?"

"No she is not."

"Okay. Why is she not aware?"

"Oh, well I haven't seen fit to…I had planned to change the will, to incorporate some of my immediate family into the will and Trudi explained to me that she would change the will any way I wanted it. All I had to do was just to tell her."

"Did you know that Trudy Gramazio also went by the name of 'Gertrude Bergman'?"

"No, I did not."

"At present, you have signed giving Trudi access to all of your assets in the bank and otherwise. Did you do this because you trust her?"

"That is correct."

"Back in March, did Trudi tell you that she wanted to buy the business, Extended Nursing Services, and did she tell you that the owner of the business was Gertrude Bergman?"

"That's right."

"Okay. Were you aware before today that Trudi is Gertrude Bergman?"

"I'm not...I was not aware of that before today.....I was under the impression that she worked for Mrs. Bergman."

"When you lent her the $20,000, what was the agreement?"

"She would furnish nursing services at no cost. I would interpret that as wholesale or no profit."

"Sam, have you been aware that she's been charging you on a weekly basis for her services, which comes out to about $70,000 a year?"

"No."

"Do you like Trudi?"

"Yes I do."

"And you trust her?"

"I do."

"Do you want to see Trudi go to jail?"

"No I don't."

"Do you understand that she has deceived you in the several matters that we just talked about?"

"Yes, yes."

"Do you want to prosecute her for the monies taken from you without your knowledge?"

"Negative."

"Do you still feel that you can trust Trudi?"

"I would raise a question mark, in all fairness to myself and to my wife, with this revelation coming as it does. There's a flag there that says, 'caution.'"

"Does your wife, Hildegard, like Trudi?"

"Yes, I think so. She likes Trudi."

After Sam's statement concluded, I went to his wife Hildegard for another interview opportunity and possible statement. I braced myself, walked into her room and gently began to greet her. Again, she began to scream in a manic, shrill voice that sent me back out the door in seconds. It was all so frustrating. One confused victim acknowledged being deceived but said that he still "trusts," yet there's also a "flag that says caution." The other victim just screamed in complete fear at my presence.

I wondered if I was traveling down the wrong road, overstepping my bounds, interfering with the rights of others. If the Brewers wanted to give every penny they had to their cat, who was I to intrude?

I headed back to the station. Gramazio's interview was coming up in a couple of hours and if she was deceptive then at least that would give me a playing field where I felt comfortable.

Trudi Gramazio appeared in casual dress. She was an attractive, middle-aged woman who appeared very pleasant, if quite talkative. She repeated that the whole matter was a misunderstanding and continually threw around names of politicians and leaders of reputable organizations and corporations as character references. She agreed to give me a statement if that would clear the matter up and we soon got into it.

The following are significant portions of the statement -- verbatim at times and paraphrased when necessary, but all of it accurate:

"Trudi, who owns Extended Nursing Services?"

"The Berglands, my mother and aunt, Gertrude and Nella. Gertrude is now deceased."

"How long has she been deceased?"

"At least 8 or 9 years, 10 years. It's been a long time."

"Mr. Brewer gave you $20,000 to purchase Extended Nursing Services. Who did you purchase the business from?"

"Mrs. Nella Bergman, my mother."

"How did you pay her the $20,000?"

"In cash. She took it. She came all the way down from her home in Pennsylvania."

"Okay. In addition to the $20,000, there are other checks for $8,000 and $5,000?"

"Yes. Sam gave them to me as a gift."

"Is Sam aware that he's paying you $1,000 and $1,400 a week for healthcare?"

"Yes. We had reached an agreement and he asked me to take that. Sam asked me to do everything. There's nothing wrong with Sam."

"Is it true that you're now the beneficiary on their will?"

"Well, it goes to charities and to me."

"And to you?"

"Right. He asked me to pick out the charity, and I'm sure there won't be anything left after that."

"So you are the beneficiary in the will then?"

"Yes."

"And is your name also on their $100,000 certificate of deposit?"

"Yes."

"Tell me what you can about Hildegard."

" It's all mental with Hildegard and she is a very jealous woman. Sam was sick of being taken care of around the clock, but she wanted a nurse too, to bathe her and whatever. Then all of a sudden she said that she couldn't walk and we'd call in a therapist. He would start to work with her and I would hold her and say, 'Come on, I know you can walk, get up, get up, get up', but she wouldn't do it. I called Doctor Carpenter and he said there's nothing wrong with her. It's all mental. She just wants to be waited on."

"So would you say she could walk?"

"Not any more, now. She's kept herself in that state too long."

"Is she competent or incompetent in your opinion?"

"I think at this point she is incompetent."

"How long in your opinion has she been incompetent? Months?"

"No, only in the last, uh...maybe 30 days. The girls started telling me that she was telling Sam he wasn't her husband."

After a series of questions regarding the "whens and wheres" of events, the interview concluded and I was truly amazed at Gramazio's performance. Sincere or not, she covered just about every base with a statement that was entirely self-serving. She asked me if everything was cleared up but I became intentionally vague, assuring her that I would be getting in touch after some further investigation.

The following morning I was told that the chief of police wanted to see me in his office. He sat behind his desk with a sincere smile when I walked in, but I still couldn't help feeling intimidated. I realized then that this was the first time in my half-dozen years as a police officer that I was in that room. Chief Joe Gerwins had a good reputation for being a fair player. Having risen through the ranks himself, he was the "cops cop," so to speak. He began talking before I could bid him a good morning.

"How are you, Joe? Have a seat." He leaned back in his chair, placed his hand on his chin and got right to the point. "Tell me about the Gramazio investigation. Just a quick summary will do."

"Well sir, this type of fraud is a little different than most. The statute's called exploitation of the elderly and ..." I gave him the scenario.

When I was done, Gerwins dropped his hand from his chin and leaned forward on his desk with a smile.

"So when the senator's wife, and the sheriff's wife, and a congressman all called me to say that this Gramazio lady is the 'salt of the earth,' it's more like 'salt on a wound', eh?"

I felt the tension go and sighed with quiet relief as he continued.

"Joe, evidently this Trudi Gramazio spends much of her time bumping elbows at political dinners, stuff like that. So the wives of some 'somebodies' called to put in a good word for her. You go ahead and treat this investigation like you would any other, and I'll call these people back and assure them that you're one of my best and you'll be fair and professional throughout this thing. Handle this with caution, be fair, and keep up the good work," the chief said

"Thank you, sir." I got up and walked out feeling good about that "cop's cop" sitting behind the desk.

Gramazio wasn't finished in her efforts to end the investigation. The following day she called, apologized for being evasive during her interview and asked to come in to clarify some things. When she arrived, she agreed to give another taped statement:

"Trudi, as I have explained to you, allegations are that you schemed to defraud the Brewers of their assets over the past year. Let's get right to the point. Who owns Extended Nursing Services?"

"Gertrude Berglin"

"Are you Gertrude Berglin?"

"Yes. That is my maiden name. I own the company."

"But why would you make it appear that 'Gertrude' was another person?"

"It would enable me to play the 'third party' when dealing with customers who wanted a cheaper rate. I could tell them that I would have to check with the owner."

"Is it true that you are the beneficiary in the Brewers' will? "

"Yes, if there is anything left but there probably won't be. Sam only has $140,000 left."

I started to ask a question, but Gramazio suddenly became irate and cut me off.

"Let me just finish one second! This is important. Sam and I got very close, as in getting close like father and daughter. I don't normally do this with my clients, but it just happened that way. Their will stated that the bank would get everything and give it to charities, but Sam didn't want that anymore. He said, 'Trudi, I want you to have it."

"Was Hildegard's signature necessary on the new will?"

"She signed it and Sam asked me to steady her hand."

"Was Hildegard competent when she signed the new will two months ago?"

"Yes, she was."

"Have you anything to add before we end this statement?"

"Yes I do. I have a reputation in town, I give more than I take, and you can verify that with all the names of the people that I've been throwing at you. I haven't done anything to Sam and he knows it. We are very close."

After the statement ended, Gramazio wanted to know where she stood in the investigation. Was she going to be arrested? Was the matter cleared up? I told her the truth: I would present the case to the prosecutor's office for their decision on criminal charges but it didn't look good.

If you ever want to get a chuckle from a cop, tell him that you want to "swear out a warrant on someone." It's not realistic, a line overused by Hollywood.

Generally, there are three different ways that a person can be charged with a felony in the state of Florida. The first would be with an actual arrest warrant that is prepared by the police and the prosecutor's office after something called "probable cause," meaning that sufficient evidence has been obtained. The warrant is then presented to a judge for review and the judge weighs the evidence to decide if he will sign it or not.

The second way is when a police officer makes an actual "probable cause arrest" at the scene of a crime. The officer usually makes this type of arrest to stop the crime, protect the community or prevent escape by the suspect. And the third way is the "arrest by capias" method, which is similar to the arrest warrant except that a prosecutor, rather than a judge, signs the capias after reviewing the case and evidence.

Gramazio was arrested the third way – by capias. The prosecutor's office agreed that both of the Brewers lacked the capacity to give consent regarding their financial matters and that Trudi had taken advantage of their infirmities, dependency and trust. In August, 1990 she was charged with Financial Exploitation of the Elderly and Organized Fraud. She surrendered without incident.

I assumed that was the end of Trudi Gramazio and the Brewers. I was wrong.

In December, just a few months after the arrest, I was contacted by out-of-state relatives of the Brewers who had just come to town. Apparently Gramazio bonded out shortly after I arrested her and returned to the Brewers' to continue "providing care."

In November, she took it upon herself to bring Sam to a new doctor, where he fell in the doctor's office and broke his hip. He was hospitalized as a result and, during his hospitalization, Gramazio wrote more than $8,000 worth of checks from his account to pay her daughter's school tuition, utilities and other bills. The Brewers' long-time personal physician said that Sam was not competent or capable of acknowledging those transactions during the hospital stay. All of this happened while Gramazio was awaiting her January trial date for the first arrest.

Hildegard Brewer's out-of-state relatives had found the processed checks in the Brewers' home. Remarkably, the attention and care of these relatives started Hildegard on the road to recovery. It was a wonderful surprise to go to the house and find this elderly lady sitting up in a wheelchair, smiling and appearing so much better.

Although she couldn't remember me, Hildegard was very cordial and more than willing to give me a taped statement.

"Hildegard, would you tell me your full name, and when your date of birth is?"

"I usually go by my mother's maiden name, Hildegard Sterling Brewer. I was born in 1905, the 31st of March."

"You're aware that Trudi Gramazio will not be coming back here. I give you my word on that. What are your feelings towards Trudi?"

"I just don't have any feelings at all because she paid no attention to me and kept me in the dark about everything.."

"Did you ever want to get out of bed?"

"Oh, of course. I'm a very ... a person who likes to move around."

"Were you aware that Trudi had dismissed Dr. Carpenter this past year from being your family doctor?"

"She told me that my doctor had retired."

"One day this year Trudi asked you to sign a document and she guided your hand as you signed the document. Were you aware that you signed a will?"

"No. She told me it was for something very important and she named it, but I forget what she said."

"Do you want Trudi to have any of your assets or monies?"

"Never. I didn't want any part of her. She ignored me."

"How do you feel towards the caretaker Marcia Cambell?"

"I love her dearly. She did everything for me. When she left, I cried."

"Did you ever try to tell anybody about the fact that Trudi had isolated you and left you alone?"

"No, I never did."

"And why not?"

"I thought I better keep quiet. I felt I was a hostage."

"Hildegard, if Trudi had taken your money without your and Sam's knowledge, would you want her to go to jail or do you just want her to go away?"

"...I'm undecided."

Hildegard's responses were remarkable. She spoke with certainty and touched the emotions of everyone in the room. As a result, I moved as quickly as possible and Gramazio was arrested again the following day. A judge increased her bond from $5,000 to $100,000.

This was finally the end of Trudi Gramazio's relationship with the Brewers. Sam stayed in the hospital and Hildegard stayed in the loving care of her family.

It was right about this time when I decided that one day I would write a book to send an important message to others. (Okay it took 10 years.)

It is not deception but disabilities that make the elderly defenseless against financial abuse. I'm sure that like many other victims, both Sam and Hildegard Brewer were quite intelligent and able to protect themselves in their younger days. But when they lost that ability through the natural aging process they became "sitting ducks" for tragedy. These victims did not become less intelligent; they just lost their ability to use the knowledge that they had. While still able, independent senior citizens must prepare for their future by making sure that someone else will be watching over their assets when they no longer can.

CHAPTER 4

BAD MEDICINE

December 1990

We drove quietly down the 600 block of 4 Key Drive with just two unmarked cars and one patrol unit.

It wasn't exactly a formal raid but more of an "inspection" after neighborhood complaints originally brought code inspectors to the house. The constant stream of ambulances and cars with out-of-state tags first attracted curiosity and then created irritation among residents of this upscale neighborhood that was nestled along the sparkling Intracoastal Waterway.

A dozen cars were parked on the lawn and by the curb of the house now. The patrolman turned on his overhead flashers as our entire group – a few detectives, two patrolmen and a code inspector – walked together to the front door.

I peered through a small window next to the door and could see a short hallway leading to what looked like a living room with several people sitting on a long couch. An attractive, Hispanic woman with jet-black hair and wearing a white nurse's uniform was bending forward, serving the people something from a tray. She glanced up at me, paused, then briskly turned and walked out of view. Things already seemed to be getting interesting.

It was quiet when I knocked. But silence isn't a good thing when a cop knocks and knows there's someone on the other side. I was just telling the patrolmen to go to the rear of the house when the door opened.

"Good afternoon, gentlemen."

A tall middle-aged man, wearing glasses, with graying brown hair stood there, smiling.

"What can I do for you?" the man asked pleasantly.

I recognized him immediately from a photo I'd seen during another investigation. His name was Lucas Boeve, a 52-year-old former Green Beret and West Point graduate.

His company, Excalibur Enterprises, was built on claims of being able to save the terminally ill through a medical treatment called "ozone therapy." The treatment was illegal, banned by the FDA. Boeve, whose degree was in engineering, was practicing medicine without a license.

Though displeased with our unexpected appearance, he allowed us in without the formalities of a search warrant. He chose that option instead of the other one: police posted at his doorstep, waiting until a warrant was obtained.

We followed him through the short hallway into a room that had a buffet table covered with various dishes of fresh fruits and raw vegetables. A group of about a dozen people, mostly elderly, was sitting quietly on couches and chairs in what appeared to be the living room.

An elderly man, a rabbi, was seated on a couch speaking in Hebrew with a young woman by his side. I greeted them and he smiled at me politely but became silent. The woman explained that she was his daughter and that he did not speak English. She said he was 80-years-old, suffering lymph cancer and they had come from Brooklyn, New York for Boeve's ozone treatments. Boeve had promised with complete confidence to cure her father and, out of desperation, they were willing to try anything. Although he didn't have much money, her father had paid $3,500 for the treatments, plus all their travel expenses.

On a couch, directly across from the rabbi, sat an elderly woman who suffered from another form of cancer and next to her was a man with AIDS, accompanied by his partner. They all gave us similar stories. Each one of them expressed enthusiasm for their progress during the treatments and a high regard for Lucas Boeve.

After the interviews, I entered an adjacent room that was apparently a dining room transformed into a treatment center. There was a large cylindrical "iron lung" type of machine on one side of the room with a woman encased inside it. Her head stuck out of one end and her feet came out the other. Through a small window, I could see water spraying around on her.

Boeve called this the "Enhancer" and explained that the woman was taking an ozone bath. It looked more like a scene from a magic show, minus the magician standing by with saw in hand, and it would have been comical if not for the tragedy of what was really happening.

On the other side of the room there was an examination table and a small meter box on wheels, with an oxygen tank and hoses attached. I had seen this gadget before, an "ozone insufflator" used to pump ozone gas into a person anally or vaginally. A wastebasket also sat nearby on the floor, full of spent syringes that Boeve had used for other treatments where he had injected ozone directly into the patient.

Ozone, or "O3," is a highly active form of oxygen. It is created when an oxygen molecule is split into two highly reactive oxygen atoms. Each of these atoms combines with another intact molecule to form the "triatomic" ozone, or "O3." When any bacteria, germ or cancer cell is directly exposed, it is killed. This is the supposed logic of ozone therapy – to pump ozone gas into a sick person's body to kill the disease.

Unfortunately, ozone is known to be extremely chemically active and it is a toxic substance in humans. There are no credible scientific reports showing the benefit of ozone and there is no valid explanation of how ozone could seek out and kill only infected cells, leaving the healthy ones unharmed. One might wonder how any person with common sense would pay for this therapy. But desperation after a terminal diagnosis, coupled with the confident promise of a cure, can often make even the most prudent persons try extreme measures in the belief they have nothing to lose.

I was kneeling over the wastebasket, poking around with my pen, when Boeve walked up.

We engaged in a verbal cat-and-mouse game. I would poke my pen in the trash, pull out a spent syringe and ask him how he administered the injections. To avoid self-incrimination, he then would play dumb, suggesting that his guests injected themselves. I continued to question him about his therapy without making much progress until we were interrupted by my partner, Bud.

"Joe, come here and take a look at this."

Bud was standing with a grin in front of a closet, holding the door open. I walked over with Boeve staying right by my side and there she was, sitting on the closet floor – that pretty Hispanic woman in the nurse's outfit.

"Lucas, why is a nurse hiding in the closet?"

He looked at me and shrugged.

"We could take you and her to the police station to pursue this."

"Look detective, wait, I apologize. This is Sabina Paz. She's Colombian and doesn't speak a word of English. She's hiding in there because she's not here legally, she's afraid of being deported. We're having a little problem getting her a work visa. I'm hoping that you can give us a break on this, just for the time being."

"A break on the illegal alien or a break on the illegal ozone therapy, Lucas?"

Boeve became very polite. He offered his total cooperation if I would forego arresting him for the moment. He said that he wanted to deal with this thing responsibly and make arrangements for his guests to return to their homes.

I still needed time to put the case together properly anyway. If I arrested him now, on probable cause, his bond would only total $2,000. But if I didn't arrest him and he fled to avoid prosecution, his bond would be revoked or raised dramatically by a judge. It didn't make sense for him to flee.

So we made an agreement. He would stop treatments immediately and close up shop in an orderly fashion, making sure his guests returned to their homes without inconvenience. And I would give him fair notice to arrange bond and surrender to me if charges were filed against him.

I was hoping that one strong motivation for Lucas Boeve not to flee would be the example of his counterpart, Basil Wainwright, who was already in jail on a $500,000 bond.

Wainwright, a 58-year-old Englishman dubbed "King Con" by the British tabloids, was a well-spoken and charismatic self-proclaimed inventor of things that either didn't work or exist. After serving a 3-year-prison term for convincing a well-known British TV personality to invest over $100,000 in a speedboat that could break the world speed record, he came to South Florida and started the Anglo American Research Company.

Wainwright was progressing from con man to exploiter of the elderly and disabled. His company's main product was the "ozone insufflator," retailing for $7,500. The insufflator would deliver ozone gas through a tube that was inserted anally or vaginally into a person. The machine supposedly would cure cancer, AIDS, Parkinson's or any other disease and the patients could even administer the treatments to themselves. But the ozone was dangerous, as were these machines, which lacked any safety mechanisms.

Finally one of Wainwright's associates, a 48-year-old female nutritional consultant, became disillusioned with his treatments and stepped forward, willing to testify against him. Wainwright had treated her for a breast condition, but she was unhappy with the results. With her testimony, a warrant was obtained and Wainwright was arrested for exploitation of the elderly and practicing medicine without a license.

He was held on a $500,000 bond because he was considered a flight risk while under investigation by the federal Immigration and Naturalization Service for his illegal residence in the country. The FDA and DPR also were investigating him.

Wainwright had sold hundreds of the machines and developed a following so strong that his bond hearing became a media circus. British reporters flew in to cover the event and one of his followers was quoted comparing his arrest to the persecution of Jesus Christ. After he was jailed, a popular radio program in Tampa made him the star of their show from his prison cell, endorsed his treatments and gave out phone numbers for those still interested in using his therapy.

I thought Lucas Boeve to be from the same mold as Wainwright. But that was a mistake because Boeve was a very different animal. Wainwright's approach to his potential victims could be described as charismatic, but Boeve's approach was aggressive.

Wainwright preferred ozone insufflation, Boeve preferred injection by needle. Wainwright liked to teach the patient self-administration and concentrated on making profits by selling machines, but Boeve tried to bring the patient under his control for ongoing treatments with up-front payments.

I soon regretted my decision not to arrest Boeve on the day of the raid. By the time I obtained a warrant for him and his "nurse," it was too late. They had fled, the house was empty and, only one week later an

AIDS victim was found abandoned and paralyzed on a dingy South Florida hotel room floor after receiving his ozone injections.

As a result, the prosecutor's office requested a bond increase, stating that Boeve was both a danger to the community and a flight risk. Fortunately, a judge granted a $1,000,000 bond to hold him if he should be arrested,but Boeve could still not be found.

A month later, my secretary dropped a fax on my desk. It was a cartoon, a simple drawing of a stork standing in a grassy marsh with its intended dinner, a frog, sticking partway out of its mouth. The frog was reaching out of the stork's beak and down around his long neck, choking the surprised bird. With an expression of determination, the frog appeared to be saying, *"Oh no buddy, I'm not going down that easy."*

Handwritten across the bottom of this cartoon were these words:

"Detective Roubicek, Thought I would brighten your day with a little humor. Regards from the D.R.! Lucas"

The sender's identifier across the top read, *"CLINIC NATURAL,* Sosua, Dominican Republic."

He was taunting me and I admit that it worked. Boeve had already relocated his clinic to a small town in the Dominican Republic and business was booming.

Attempts began to get him extradited back to Florida and a federal warrant for "Unlawful Flight to Avoid Prosecution" was obtained. The FBI worked diligently with the Dominican government and, finally, the local police took him into custody. But Lucas Boeve had been scoring points with members of the Dominican government, providing ozone therapy to a governor, a sheriff, and the sheriff's wife. When he was transported to the airport to be flown to the states, the Dominican military was waiting and forced his release.

The final tragic story to come from Boeve's ozone therapy emerged one year later, in March 1992. A grief-stricken and very angry mother, Peggy Delegar, called me from Pan American Hospital in Miami, where her 27-year-old daughter, Kelly, had just been admitted after being flown in from Boeve's clinic. Kelly had been diagnosed with lymph cancer only two months earlier. Her American doctors had sent her home from the hospital with a grim diagnosis – she was given just six months to live.

Someone had recommended that Kelly check out Boeve's "miracle treatments." She was desperate, so she did.

After speaking by phone with Boeve, she was ecstatic because he had given her hope. Her mother, Peggy, had strong reservations and resisted Kelly's pleas to go, but how many times could she look her terminally ill child in the eyes and say, "It won't work"?

In February 1992, Kelly Delegar was flown to Boeve's *Clinic Natural*, accompanied by her mother. Boeve demanded $12,000 in cash upfront and he got it.

At first, Kelly was impressed with the country club/spa atmosphere of the clinic, but things quickly went downhill and her condition worsened. Her daily diet consisted only of fresh fruits and vegetables and she lost weight dramatically. Her treatments involved daily ozone injections by needle, but her mother soon realized that conditions were unsanitary and there were no medical doctors on the premises.

Kelly needed help quickly and her mother confronted Boeve, demanding answers and action. But Boeve only saw a new adversary rather than a desperate mother who was trying to save her child. He had her escorted off the property at gunpoint by his bodyguards.

Only with help from the American Consulate was she able to retrieve her daughter, eventually flying Kelly to Miami and then to Pan American Hospital.

But Peggy Delegar wasn't calling me now because of the close call at *Clinic Natural*. She was calling because her daughter had just died.

Months later, the TV news program, *NBC Dateline*, carried a special report on the incident. I sat at home and watched Lucas Boeve on television, giving a guided tour of Clinic Natural to the reporter.

He professed the legitimacy of ozone as the cure-all for every disease known. He claimed to have cured Magic Johnson of AIDS. He claimed that Kelly's family brought her to his clinic to die as part of a government conspiracy to get him out of the country. He claimed that the pharmaceutical companies stood to lose billions of dollars if his therapy were legalized. He calmly lied to the camera, over and over.

I watched Peggy Delegar weep as she told her story. She recalled her daughter crying, *"Please don't leave me, Mommy! Please don't leave me!"* as she was escorted off the property at gunpoint.

I imagined myself in her position, my child in *Clinic Natural*, and the thought made me sick. I listened as the report ended with the news that Kelly Delegar didn't die at Pan American Hospital of cancer. She died of blood poisoning. Lucas Boeve had killed Kelly Delegar with an infection. Her terminal illness is irrelevant – there is no way now to know how much longer she might have lived.

"Lucas crossed a line that you just don't cross. He gave Kelly hope and took her dignity. For what? A few dollars? There are some things you just don't do," her mother had said during the television report.

In just a few words, she nailed the entire ozone therapy movement. Giving hope and taking dignity, for a few dollars.

After the *NBC Dateline* story, the FBI made another serious attempt at getting Boeve out of the Dominican. This time the military took him into custody and an FBI agent called me while they were en route to the airport to fly him to San Juan, Puerto Rico and then to Miami. I was heading to Miami International Airport to take custody after his arrival but I got a second call from the FBI.

This time, before Lucas had boarded the plane in the Dominican Republic, the police had forced the military to release him. Lucas was a free man again and to the day of this writing he has not been captured.

As for Basil Wainwright? After serving his sentence in federal prison, he established a significant following in Kenya, which has the seventh highest AIDS fatality rate in the world, with more than 1.2 million people presently infected.

In July 1996, the Director of Medical Services in Nairobi, Kenya publicly congratulated Wainwright on his ozone therapy and assured him of government support for what would likely be a "medical breakthrough for Kenya." Winnie Mandela, ex-wife of Nelson Mandela, also publicly supported him while she was visiting the country.

But by July 1998, Wainwright's therapy was banned by the health minister, who proclaimed that it was "endangering the lives of Kenyans and exposing them to fraud."

Wainwright quickly fled the country and, like Boeve, remains at large.

There are no proven cases of ozone therapy curing any terminal disease. Every victim that I dealt with, people who believed the therapy "at least gave hope," had to later deal with the reality that it was a false hope.

These "bad medicine" cases differed from my prior cases because they involved victim's being exploited through their physical disabilities. They illustrate a victim impact that reaches far beyond financial injury, putting exploitation into its proper perspective. Still, exploitation cases are classified and treated as "property crimes," like fraud, by most government agencies. The misleading result is that the victim impact of a property crime is measured only by the dollar amount of the victim's loss.

Tell that to Kelly Delegar's mom.

CHAPTER 5

THE MCNEELY RESIDENCE

January, 1991

As soon as they kicked open the front door they saw her on the floor, lying in her own waste, covered with ants.

She had been there for days, abandoned and alone. Sunlight narrowly cut through the otherwise dark living room, focusing on her broken frame like an intense spotlight as paramedics rushed to her side and police officers walked cautiously by on a routine search of adjacent rooms. At the hospital, she was diagnosed as suffering from several broken ribs, severe dehydration and acute psychosis. A CAT scan revealed atrophy of the brain.

She could tell the police and paramedics her name, Sarah McNeely, but that was all, and the evidence suggested that she simply fell while unattended. The neighbor who called police to the scene that day cast suspicion on a young man named Gregory who claimed to be her caretaker, but Gregory hadn't been seen by anyone for a couple of weeks. A Porsche was tucked beneath a car cover and parked in Sarah's driveway. The vehicle's registration came back to a man named "Gregory McNeely." A picture of the 36-year-old businessman sat on Sarah's television set.

Days later, Donna Hewitt, the neighbor that had called the police to rescue Sarah, gave a formal statement that indicated that Gregory may have been taking advantage of her.

"Mrs. Hewitt, what happened on the day that you called the police?"

Well, I hadn't seen Sarah's lights on or any activity in her house for the past couple of days. Normally I hear her opening the door and talking to the neighborhood cats that she feeds, but nothing. I walked over and could hear moaning coming from inside, so I went by the window and said, 'Sarah, are you okay?' and she said, 'Yes. I'm okay.' I asked her to come to the door but she said that she couldn't, so that's when I called the police.

"Could you give me your opinion on Sarah's mental well-being for the past year?"

I've known Sarah for the past 15 years and she was a very sharp woman, but for the past year and a half she has been very confused.

"Could you give me an example?"

Well, sometimes she would come outside and walk up to me and say, 'Donna is that you? Is that you, Donna?' She would do the same with my children.

"What can you tell me about Gregory McNeely?"

Well, he started mowing her lawn about a year and a half ago and I know that he wanted her house, but she absolutely did not want to give her house to anyone.

"Have you ever actually been in contact with Gregory McNeely?"

Yes. Gregory came over and told me that Sarah was very upset because she saw me standing on her property. We were redoing our house at the time and she was concerned that we were building on her property. He said, 'You know you ought to be nicer to her. You have a rich old lady living next to you.' I was so enraged I said, 'What does her financial situation have to do with anything?' That incident led me to believe that he had more interests than helping a little old lady.

"Is there anything else?"

Yes, a couple of months ago when I was cleaning my pool, I heard Gregory in the back of the house telling someone that he wanted to have the roof redone and French doors put on, but he wasn't going to do that until she was dead. And those were his exact words.

Sarah's rescue and her neighbor's statement kicked off a criminal investigation that ultimately led to Gregory McNeely's arrest. The following is a summary of the evidence obtained, including significant portions of statements taken during the investigation.

Donna Hewitt's statement led me to check into the ownership of Sarah's house and her bank accounts. The surprising result was not just the asset transfer that already had occurred but also the extent of that transfer.

Only three months earlier, Gregory had gained legal title to Sarah's house, valued at $200,000 at the time, by having her sign a quit claim deed. He also had Sarah sign power of attorney over to him and then had placed his name on her $35,000 certificate of deposit and all of her bank accounts. He rapidly depleted her accounts, cashed in the certificate of deposit and took out a home equity loan on the house for $75,000.

I also learned that Gregory owned the Oceanside Gym, a fitness center located right beside the famous Fort Lauderdale beach. When I stopped by, the manager said that Gregory was out of state on vacation but was expected back in a couple of weeks. By now, Fort Lauderdale police officers had towed the Porsche from Sarah's driveway and stored it. I attached a message to the car, asking my colleagues to contact me when Gregory turned up.

I had many questions to answer before even thinking about arresting this supposed caretaker. Was Gregory McNeely related to Sarah McNeely, or was he just using the coincidence of the same last name as an opportunity? Did Gregory take any measures to ensure the proper care of Sarah whenever he left her alone? As her caretaker, he was legally required to do so. Most importantly, did Sarah truly consent to the massive transfer of her assets to this man and did she have the mental capacity to give that consent at the time?

There were almost no medical records to flesh out her story. No family physician, no visits to any doctor's office. The only files available were those filled out in the emergency room on the day of her rescue. But by knocking on doors throughout her neighborhood, I was able to track down witnesses who finally helped to provide more answers.

Fred Neubeiser was another neighbor who gave me a statement, offering important information about both Sarah and Gregory.

"Mr. Neubeiser, would you say that Sarah has been competent the past couple of years?"

"No, I wouldn't. She would come over for help repeatedly in making small decisions. Just a couple of weeks before the police came, she was asking me to explain her newspaper bill. I would read it to her

three times and seconds later she would forget what I had said. She
cannot concentrate."

"How long has she been like that?"

"For about the past two years now."

"How does she get around?"

"She has a walker that she uses all the time but her movement is
very limited. We get her newspaper and put it at her door because she
has such difficulty getting to it. Other than coming to neighbors for help,
she doesn't leave her home."

"How about Gregory? Was there ever any problem with him?"

"Normally Gregory would let us know when he went away. He
would stop by and tell us that he bought her some food and how long he
would be gone, but this time he didn't say anything. I was very
disappointed in him. We realized that he was gone when Sarah came to
our house asking me to get her some food."

"Has Sarah ever given you any monies or gifts?"

"No, but if she had she wouldn't even have realized that it was
gone. That's how bad she was."

Millie Hertner was an old friend of Sarah's who had gotten Sarah
home health aides to assist her in her home over a year earlier, due to
Sarah's infirmities. During an interview with me, I asked whether she
thought that Sarah had been able to take care of herself at the time of the
asset transfer to Gregory.

I may as well have asked her if Sarah could fly.

"No. That's why I hired the nurses. She can barely walk, barely
see with cataracts and she's confused. She would constantly call me

over to explain her bills and taxes, then she would have me repeat it over and over again. She's been this way for a couple of years."

Another friend, William Williams, confirmed much of the information provided by others, but also mentioned to me a new document that Sarah had recently shown him.

"It was this new will that she had signed and Sarah wanted to know what I thought of it. I asked her if she really intended to give everything to Gregory McNeely and she said, 'Who's that?' I said, ' The nice young man that does your lawn,' and she says, 'Oh no, certainly not!'"

Jean Coburn, the loan officer at Sarah's bank, did not beat around the bush in her statement to me. She explained that Gregory had been to the bank in late November to close on the $75,000 home equity loan.

"He said that she was his grandmother and he was fixing up the house for her. He claimed that she was recovering from a broken hip. But he convinced her that she didn't need the nurses and got her up out of bed and they exercised together. He also claimed that they walked together to our branch on the Causeway about a mile from her home."

"Did you ever meet Sarah McNeely?"

"No. He said that she was doing great though, walking a mile every day."

"Were you suspicious of Gregory?"

"Yes, from day one. When someone wants cash and takes a penalty on a CD and comes in every couple of days wanting cash, cash, cash, with a different story? I thought he was just ripping his grandmother off. Afterwards when I saw a copy of the quit claim deed, I realized that it

was done on the same day that the power of attorney was implemented on the CDs."

The loan officer believed that she was legally bound to honor the documents despite her suspicions that Gregory was ripping off his grandmother. As of this writing (and after many lawsuits), banks are more cautious when exploitation is suspected. New laws specifically give them the authority to refuse asset transfer and report suspected exploitation.

Sarah McNeely was recovering nicely by now so I thought it prudent to take a statement while her physical condition allowed it. An interview with Sarah at least would help document her lack of mental capacity during her statement to me.

I found her in a nursing home, lying in bed.

"Sarah, could you tell me how old you are?"

"Well, I'm 91 plus ... "

"Okay, could you tell me your date of birth?"

"February the ... 24th...19-something"

"Eighteen ninety-nine maybe?"

"Eighteen ninety-nine, yes."

"Sarah, do you remember if you gave Gregory your house in the will?"

"I don't know, I ... "

Sarah looked at me silently.

"Sarah, do you have trouble remembering things?"

Silence.

"Sarah, do you know what power of attorney is?"

"No, I'm not up on those legal questions."

"Do you know that you gave Gregory permission to sign your name on your checks and have access to your bank accounts?"

"No, I didn't."

"Did you give Gregory permission to do anything?"

"He kept the grounds in order, that's all. I did not give him permission to just go in and sign my name to anything."

Her inability to understand and answer very basic questions was obvious and would have been just as obvious to Gregory when he was having her sign over ownership of her every asset.

The one critical piece of evidence I still needed in this investigation was a statement from Gregory McNeely himself. That came on February 12th when he returned to town.

He called me, not to ask about Sarah's rescue, but because he wanted his Porsche back. When I returned his call at the gym he was very patronizing but agreed to come to the police station to explain everything in a formal statement. He even brought the new will with him.

"Gregory, are you Sarah's caretaker?"

"Yes, I've been taking care of her for four years."

"Did you do anything to make sure that she was taken care of in your absence, maybe even ask someone to keep an eye on her?"

"Oh yeah detective, she was 100 percent when I left. She was in great shape or I wouldn't have left her. I tell you, back when she had her accident and went to the hospital, they put her in rehab and then they put her in a nursing home to die. But I went up there and got her on her

feet. I got her walking up and down the aisles. I mean, she did a total
about-face."

"Did you tell anyone at all that you were going away and ask them
to watch her?"

"Yeah, the neighbors across the street, the Neubeisers."

"How did you meet Sarah?"

"I had an acquaintance that lived on the same street as Sarah. One
day while passing, I saw Sarah lying on her lawn. I stopped and helped
her up and as I was walking back to my car she says, 'By the way,
what's your name, sir?' I said that my name was Gregory McNeely and
started walking back to my car again and she said, 'You look like a
McNeely.' I turned around and looked at her and asked her what that's
supposed to mean and then she told me her name. Well, I told her that it
was a pleasure to meet her and that's how our relationship began."

"Gregory, could you please explain how your relationship evolved
to being Sarah's caretaker and beneficiary in her will?"

"Absolutely. In the beginning she fired a couple of people that she
was paying to take care of her lawn and she asked me to do it. At first I
said, 'Sarah, I don't have the equipment to do this and I'm pretty busy. I
own the Oceanside Gym, the Oceanside Motel, the Southbeach Market
and I lease out other stores,' but you know I did it anyway. After that,
she said, 'You have to do it or I'll let the grass grow up to the windows.'
So I went out and bought the lawn mower, edger and trimmers and said,
'Okay, I'll do it.'"

"Gregory, are you getting anything in Sarah's will?"

"Yep, the house – the house and her assets. I've got a copy of it with me. She gave the will to me because she didn't want anyone to see it. She was so intent that she wanted this house in my name before I left. I said, 'Sarah, what's the big deal? My name is in the will. What's the difference?' And she said, 'According to living trust, they can take 15 to 20 percent of my assets before it goes into probate and I don't want anybody giving you trouble on the house. That's what I want and that's all there is to it.'"

My jaw dropped when he quoted Sarah. He made her sound like my accountant, but smarter.

"She sounds like she was a smart woman a few months ago. Was she capable of paying the bills herself back then?"

"She was. Yes, I'd say she was."

"Is she now?"

"I don't know."

There's an old saying, "The easiest way to be cheated is to believe yourself to be smarter than others." I think that Gregory believed that he was covering his tracks, but unwittingly provided witness to the asset transfer from Sarah to himself, something that Sarah couldn't do.

After an emergency guardianship hearing was arranged for Sarah, her nephew flew in from out of state to become her official guardian. She stayed in the nursing home because of her failing condition.

I turned over my evidence to a special prosecutor who handled only elderly abuse cases. Felony charges of exploitation of the elderly, neglect of the elderly with injury and first-degree grand theft were filed against Gregory McNeely. The charges were serious and prison would be certain if he were convicted of all of them.

Gregory surrendered without incident and quickly bonded out on that same day for just $12,000. I was stunned by the ease of his release.

In Florida, a defendant's attorney can take depositions as part of the discovery process, which is that phase of a court case when the defense can learn what evidence the state has beyond the filing documents. When I was deposed for this case, two reputable attorneys were present to represent Gregory. This worried me. More than one defense attorney at a deposition normally means that the police officer will be harassed with endless unreasonable questions. But that was not what happened.

The process began with some routine questions that I already had clearly answered in the police report and then, almost as quickly as it began, the deposition was over. The lead attorney advised me that he had no more questions. I could go. It was almost a pleasant experience. I wondered if our case was that strong – or perhaps I was missing something.

I was.

The prosecutor later told me that he was seriously considering a deal offered by the defense. The defense attorneys had argued that there was neither expert testimony nor any medical record that proved Sarah lacked adequate mental capacity when she signed the papers giving her assets to Gregory. As a result, the defense could simply request a "Motion To Dismiss" hearing before the presiding judge, knowing they had a strong chance of getting the charges thrown out.

Judge Susan Lebow, known by her detractors as "Let'em Go Lebow," was presiding and if she tossed out the case, Sarah would be completely destitute, with absolutely no assets. The defense was offering a deal where Gregory would pay Sarah the fair market value for her home. In return, the state would drop all charges.

I was in shock. There was an abundance of expert testimony and medical records proving that Sarah clearly lacked capacity in January, but the prosecutor did not want to take any chances. Although Sarah's neighbors would not have been allowed to give their opinions on her mental capacity, they still could testify to her short-term memory loss – specific events such as Sarah asking her neighbor to explain the newspaper bill repeatedly or strange comments such as walking up to a friend of 15 years and asking, "Donna, is that you?" I was disappointed because I believed and still believe that this was a strong case.

Some might say that the prosecutor had a responsibility to pursue a conviction simply based on the nature of this case, but there was real merit to his concerns. Judge Lebow had earned a well-deserved reputation for throwing out cases based on what many cops and prosecutors considered an unconventional interpretation of the law. Several years after Sarah's case, Lebow would receive national attention for overturning a jury's guilty verdict in a manslaughter case against NFL player Brian Blades and later she dismissed a drug charge against a gay man for a truly bizarre reason: Lebow decided the undercover officer entrapped the gay man by being too good looking. In fairness to the judge, her rulings may have been correct but her reputation still gave understandable pause to prosecutors.

On February 6, 1992, all three felony charges against Gregory McNeely were dropped and he paid Sarah, through her legal guardian, the fair market value for the house. Sarah's neighbors began calling me to ask why Gregory was back working on the yard and I felt ashamed when I told them. The prosecutor actually had a reputation for being aggressive with exploitation cases but later told me that he was growing weary of it all. The struggle to win convictions in these difficult cases was too much. He left the state Attorney's Office about a year later.

The bottom line here is that Sarah McNeely's house became Gregory's simply because she had signed a few documents and the caretaker had insisted that this forgetful, elderly lady had wanted to do so. Despite all the evidence to the contrary, the state believed that prosecutors might not have been able to prove otherwise.

Although many of my exploitation cases ended with arrests, convictions and prison terms, others fell to the wayside because of capacity and consent issues that still plague prosecution efforts today. If Sarah's lack of capacity had already been documented before Gregory met her, it would have been a moot point and this case would have been a strong one.

CHAPTER 6

BILLS FOR BUD

January 1994

How odd for him to be propped in front of his window like a puppet, to be treated in such an undignified manner after an honorable lifetime of helping others. He could recite by long-term memory his favorite poems by Kipling and Dickinson, or tell survival stories from the days of the Great Depression when he found odd jobs to support his parents and siblings, but because of acute short-term memory loss he couldn't recall the day, month or even year. If you asked, he'd just crack you a smile and say that he didn't bother with those things anymore.

How unfortunate that 95-year-old Bud Witt would be looking at his visiting out-of-state relative while his supposed "caretaker" hoisted him to the window by his belt. Bud could only communicate through the muffling glass. In a hoarse, calm voice, he assured his visitors that everything was just fine, but he refused to open the door. Instead, he politely asked them to leave.

Standing in the yard were his cousin, Shirley Mosholder, her husband and a police officer. The Mosholders were looking at the officer in disbelief because, despite their pleas, he refused to force entry into Bud's home or order Bud and his companion out.

Shirley tried reasoning with the patrol cop.

"C'mon officer, doesn't this look suspicious? You don't think something's wrong here? Bud's almost a hundred years old, he doesn't know what the hell is going on!"

The patrolman sympathized, but wouldn't budge.

"Miss, I'm sorry, but he just said that everything's fine and he doesn't appear to be in distress. You said yourself that the old man's been telling you on the phone that these are his friends and everything's okay. He's not asking for help and I can't just kick the door in because you feel suspicious. If he changes his tune or something new happens give us a call, but at the moment I can't help you."

The Mosholders had driven all the way to Fort Lauderdale, Florida in January 1994 from their home in Pennsylvania because they suspected that two renters in the apartment building Bud owned had been taking advantage of him. Whenever Shirley called to check on her cousin, either Bob Cote or his girlfriend, Delores Rizzo, would answer and say that he was napping or at a doctor's appointment. On the rare occasion that Bud answered, he insisted that everything was fine but seemed confused and disoriented. Shirley knew that age was taking its toll on him and anyone, specifically Cote and Rizzo, could take advantage if they desired. She suspected that they were turning "care" into "control" for personal gain. But what she didn't know was the condition and safety of Bud's assets. At the moment she could only point a finger at this couple and call them suspicious.

Cote and Rizzo had been renting an apartment from Bud for several years, but over time Bud lost the capacity to manage his finances, so they had taken over completely. By their admission, they managed his apartment building, collected the rents, paid all the bills, cleaned, and cooked his meals. They "assisted" him with major financial decisions, including the sale and refinancing of his properties for extra cash. Cote would later say that Bud insisted on buying him a new Corvette but that the rest of the cash had gone to pay Bud's bills.

It didn't look that way. While Bud was under the "care" of Cote and Rizzo, the house next door that he once had owned was sold for $90,000 and that money was completely gone now. Rent money was collected by Cote but never made it to Bud's bank. The financial accounts of this old man who survived the Great Depression were being drained, his valuables were disappearing and arrangements already were in progress for a new home equity loan on the apartment building.

Shirley Mosholder was worried that Bud was being exploited, but she couldn't learn anything about his finances. After the patrolman drove away, she and her husband walked back to bid farewell to Bud, but he was already gone from the window. The Mosholders drove home to Pennsylvania feeling defeated and frustrated.

They would return to Fort Lauderdale one day, but of course it would be too late. By then, Bud would be another statistic.

Four months after the Mosholders went home, the closing took place for a $90,000 home equity loan on Bud's apartment building – at 16 ½ percent interest. That a loan with such a colossal interest rate was given to a 95-year-old man should have sent up warning flags. But the attorney who handled the closing later explained that he believed Bud had the mental capacity to manage his own financial matters. Of course, that attorney profited from the closing.

Under the "care" of Cote and Rizzo, Bud was nearing the point where he would be completely penniless. It sounded like the same broken record: a victim who gives permission but lacks capacity, an attorney who claims the victim had capacity but almost certainly knew better. And inaction by the government due to lack of experience and training. There was an exploitation law, but even that was about to be overhauled and seriously compromised.

June 1994 was a period of unexpected changes for Florida's laws dealing with crimes against the elderly. I had been hearing for months about a new, tougher elderly crimes law that was under consideration. A special legislative session now was in progress in Tallahassee, the state capital, and lawmakers were working on the measure.

Unfortunately, I didn't actually read the proposed law until June 9, when it was ready for a vote by legislators. That's when I saw a significant problem.

I felt there was a crucial wording error that could make the exploitation section of the bill inapplicable to more than 2 million Florida senior citizens. Under the "penalties" section of the statute, the word "and" was used in place of the word "or" in a crucial sentence:

"… A person who knowingly exploits an elderly person by the improper or illegal use or management of the assets, power of attorney, *and* guardianship of such elderly person for profit, commits a felony in the third degree."

The word "and" made it a requirement that the suspect have formal, court appointed guardianship over the exploitation victim.

Otherwise the law would not apply and could not be used for prosecution. If the bill passed as written, every elderly person in Florida who was not under *legal* guardianship would lose all protection against exploitation.

Elderly people like Bud Witt.

After spotting the problem, I contacted a friend, the head of the training division of the Attorney General's Office in the capital. She agreed that this was a significant issue and said that she would have someone get back to me.

As a result, the executive director of the state attorney's office in Broward County, Monica Hofheinz, called me. Monica represents the State Attorney on legislative issues. She said that she had looked into the matter and talked with some committee members who drafted the bill containing the proposed law. She wanted me to fly with her to Tallahassee early the next morning, where I would speak before the Florida House and Senate Committees that were considering this legislation.

My job, she said, was to convince them that they must not pass the exploitation portion of the bill as written.

Realistically, I couldn't just hop on a plane to Tallahassee. Department procedures had to be followed, travel forms and per diem vouchers had to be filled out and the Fort Lauderdale police chief had to give personal approval because funds for investigative expenses were tight. This was government and you don't "just do it" in government.

I also was married to another police officer who worked the same shift and we had two young kids. It's not always easy for a husband and father to "just do it" either.

Still, I told Monica that I would try to arrange the trip somehow. When approached, the chief and my wife were unhappy with the fact that I was leaving my normal responsibilities behind for a while, but in the end I got the go-ahead from the both of them and was on my way.

I sat beside Monica on the 7am flight to Tallahassee the next morning, not feeling a whole lot of enthusiasm. But I was there, nonetheless.

Apprehension is the best word to describe my emotions. Standing in public before the state's lawmakers to tell them that they were about to commit a serious blunder is the same as telling them that they were totally "screwing up." It's not what rank-and-file police officers, even detectives such as me, normally do. I knew that I had to present myself, not as a criminal investigator, but as an advocate for the elderly whose intent was only to prevent passing a law that would hurt the people it was intended to protect.

A crash course in the law-making process of Florida goes something like this. First, suggestions are made to state legislators by individuals or groups for a new law. A Senator or House member must agree to sponsor proposed legislation to create this new law. The proposed legislation then becomes a "bill". Over time there are committee meetings to make changes to the bill until it is considered finalized and ready to be voted on. After the bill is accepted and voted on by the two legislative bodies, the Senate and the House of Representatives, it is sent to the Governor for signature. Once it is signed it becomes law on the effective date of the legislation. The laws are then compiled to form Florida statutes.

That portion of the bill pertaining to crimes against the elderly was the only issue of the special session that was bipartisan, agreed to by both Democrats and Republicans. It was something positive for the legislators to hang their hats on, some clear and non-controversial accomplishment to brag about to their constituents. I was about to point out that they were going to hang their hats on a new law that would provide more protection for the predators than the victims.

When we arrived in Tallahassee, the Capitol buildings impressed me. There were four main buildings that faced each other around a giant courtyard, all contained within one city block. There was the new Capitol building that included in its design a 22-story tower built in the 1970's. Directly across from this sat the old Capitol building, a historic site built in 1824, now used mainly for tours. On the opposing sides of the courtyard were the Senate and House Office Buildings that contained the offices of both legislative bodies.

When we walked through the square, I had trouble keeping up with Monica's pace. She moved so fast that I would have been lost if she had gotten away from me. In her job, she was often in the Capitol lobbying for the interests of state prosecutors and she was quite good at it. Monica was intelligent, persuasive, a master with words. When I asked her advice on what to tell the legislators, she simply said, "The truth, Joe. Be sincere, get to the point and keep it under three minutes."

Three minutes didn't sound too bad, I thought.

But before I had the chance to begin talking, I learned a quick lesson in political reality. The legislators who vote on the bills are chosen by the people of Florida to represent them. Each is responsible for making sure that those who elected him or her have a voice in all matters concerning the state. I realized that was obviously not the case when two staff members approached me in the hallway just outside the legislative chambers. They attempted to persuade me that I should not speak to the lawmakers. They were straightforward and made it very clear that the bill's wording about guardianship was not a mistake. They said it was part of an intentional plan to lower costs for both the statewide abuse registry and Adult Protective Services, the social service agency that investigated the complaints.

In other words, they were trying to make sure fewer abused elderly people could demand protection from the state! The legislature wasn't trying to protect seniors, it was trying to save money while *appearing* to protect seniors.

The abuse hotline registry was required to base its guidelines for accepting complaints of abuse, neglect and exploitation on state law. If lawmakers passed a new law that required formal guardianship for exploitation complaints, the state could turn away the majority of exploitation cases and keep the cash. Perhaps later, this restrictive wording would be corrected as if it had all been an innocent mistake. So, rather than address the financial problem in an ethical manner, a decision was made to sabotage the law instead.

The people who approached me made every effort to prevent me from speaking to legislators about the bill. One man in particular, a short slick guy wearing glasses, suspenders and a bow tie, did most of the talking. To me, he seemed a "weasel" prepared with rationalizations for the scheme.

"The elderly are already protected by the grand theft statute," he said. "We can write a new bill down the road. Don't worry, we can work together on this."

But my views were very different. I turned away from the two, walking now with Monica into the House chamber, down the long aisle towards the front. She whispered after I sat down.

"Stay here. I have some things to do. I'll probably speak before you so don't be nervous, you'll do just fine."

The proceedings continued and people approached the podium and spoke on elderly issues while the representatives and hundreds of people in the audience listened attentively. A giant screen in front of the room showed the person addressing the panel so that everyone could see the speaker close-up.

I was getting more nervous by the minute.

Eventually, Monica's name was called. She approached the podium, respectfully greeted the legislators and complimented them on their work to protect the elderly. Then she explained the wording problem with the exploitation portion of the bill. I admired her ability to carry herself and actually forgot that I was next, but someone walked up to me and whispered in my ear.

"Detective, we just want you to know that even if you fall flat on your face up there, we admire your intentions and we'll still be more than willing to work with you in the future."

It was that little weasel guy with the bow tie and suspenders. God, I wanted to trip him as he departed, but as he walked away I heard a different voice from behind me.

"Detective Roubicek, you'll do just fine, don't worry."

I turned around and there sat the state Secretary of Elder Affairs, Bentley Lipscomb. He smiled and continued.

"Some of us are aware of the problem now and a few allies are sitting up there. You'll do fine."

I thanked him, feeling both surprise and relief. Then my name was called.

Walking to the podium, I noticed an elderly woman in a wheelchair in the aisle to my left. She gave me a smile as I passed and it gave me purpose because I felt like her legitimate representative. After reminding myself of Monica's advice, "Keep it under three minutes," I introduced myself and got to the point.

"I'm here to talk about the problem with the wording of the exploitation portion of the bill and the consequences of restricting exploitations to persons under guardianship."

I quickly read aloud the proposed section requiring guardianship and continued with my remarks.

"Now, I know that Monica Hofheinz has pointed out the prosecution problems with exploitation cases, but I would like to talk about the victim impact and its magnitude, as an investigator who sees it firsthand. The law enforcement community has to deal with many demands and, unfortunately, elderly crimes can take a back seat to other needs. When exploitations are investigated, elderly victims are often poor witnesses and we cannot prosecute due to their memory loss, guilt or fear of retaliation. And the culprits walk away. The only law, the only tool that investigators have to deal with in these situations, is the exploitation statute. I traveled across the state today to ask you not to take that away, not to pass this bill in its present form."

Some people in the audience applauded. Panel members began speaking with each other and I felt confident. I decided to mention my earlier meeting in the hall.

"I have been approached here in the Capitol this morning and asked to consider budget concerns, to look at the bigger picture, before speaking. I can't do that, especially when I know that someone else won't be doing it."

I believe that I crossed a line at that point.

The chairman stepped in, commended me for my work and said that a meeting about this issue was being scheduled for that same afternoon. He thanked me for speaking and I stepped away from the podium with a great sense of relief. That was that, at least for the House.

My statement in the Senate Chambers was cancelled because a committee meeting to address the problem now was planned. About a dozen people, including a senator, attended that session. It started constructively but an agreement could not be reached on how the bill could be written to suit the needs of all parties present. The final decision was to leave the wording of the present bill alone, and create a separate section to address the criminal aspect. Police and prosecutors could use the criminal section, while the state's adult protective services division could use the other. This was how the committee meeting ended. Not the best outcome, but it seemed like something.

But soon after our return home, I found out that the special legislative session ended without passing any of the bills.

I asked Monica if our trip to Tallahassee really accomplished anything and she said that it did. The threat of losing the standing exploitation statute was over, but the process had begun to put together a new bill, a better law to protect the elderly.

On June 30, I received a letter from Secretary Bentley Lipscomb that went as follows:

"I am particularly encouraged by your successful negotiations for further improvements during the June 10th, 1994 meeting at the capitol. While it is regrettable that our elected officials did not act on this legislation, please be assured that I will ask the Governor to include Adult Protective Services in the call for any Special Sessions which may be held."

Ironically, on the same day that I received this letter, the Florida Supreme Court found the standing exploitation statute to be unconstitutionally vague and struck it down. The law's words, "the infirmities of aging," were not specific enough.

Suddenly, there was no longer a special law designed to protect people like Bud Witt. The trip to Tallahassee seemed inconsequential and efforts to make a better law appeared to be in vain.

On November 7, just a few months later, Bud Witt was knocking on his neighbor's door begging for food. He was 50 pounds lighter than he had been in January and a clothespin held up the pants on his skeletal frame. Adult Protective Services responded that same day and the Mosholders began another trip to South Florida.

They found Bud's home completely stripped. Two empty windows sat where he once had air conditioning units. The crystal chandelier was missing from the dining room and pictures were taken from the walls. An antique dish set no longer sat on its display shelf and his jewelry was gone. Several rings from Bud's home were later found at a pawnshop, sold by Bob Cote.

By this time, Bud's contact with the outside world had been completely cut off. He had no phone, radio, television or newspaper. His utility services had been turned off, or were about to be, due to lack of payment. Two paper bags full of mail, Bud's bills, were found hidden behind a shelf in the apartment building's laundry room and the foreclosure process on the building had already begun. Just as had happened with the money from his neighboring property, the proceeds of the $90,000 equity loan on the apartment building had vanished.

This is when I finally had the pleasure of meeting Bud – and taking on his case.

When I went to his house, he was sitting at a table in an empty living room wearing, of all things, a smile. He was a hell of a pleasant guy, the type that chose to see "silver linings" in the clouds. He loved words, quips and quotes and could recite poem verses by memory. The name "Witt" just seemed to fit his personality.

The irony was that, despite his ability to quote a favorite poem by Emily Dickinson, he couldn't tell you the current month, day, or year because of short-term memory loss. He obviously lacked the capacity to give legal consent about his financial matters and anyone who spoke with him for more than a few moments would have known that.

When I mentioned Bob Cote and Dorothy Rizzo, Bud's smile faded a bit. He no longer referred to them as friends. He complained that they had stopped feeding and caring for him and recalled one incident with a large white, ivory shoehorn that was sitting on the table between us. He slowly picked it up and showed it to me.

"Bob would slap this on the table, over and over in front of me and say, 'We have to get more money Bud, or I don't know what I'm gonna do.' Detective, I didn't know that my money was gone."

Bud was insistent that he absolutely did not give his assets to Cote or Rizzo, but his memory problems prevented him from recalling what really had happened. Without a law that recognized victims with disabilities, Bud would be punished rather than protected for suffering from his mental lapses. I remembered that the "weasel" in Tallahassee wasn't concerned about these issues and that a new law couldn't be passed until the next year's legislative session.

Bob Cote couldn't be found but justice was served to some extent after we discovered Delores Rizzo in the upstairs apartment that she and Cote had rented from Bud. I found a handful of Bud's returned checks that she had cashed. They had notations like "groceries" and "cleaning" on them. When questioned, Rizzo justified cashing his checks by insisting that she was Bud's caretaker, but by doing so she took responsibility for him and the condition of his home. As a result, she was arrested for elderly neglect and grand theft for taking his money without providing the agreed services.

Rizzo was arrested on November 17, with Thanksgiving just around the corner. That made a nice news angle for holiday human interest stories about a starving, abused old man. The local newspapers and television stations gave Bud's tragedy "prime time" coverage. His poetry recitations and constant smile only made him that much more endearing to those who heard of his plight. Many people soon gave Bud, this old man with nothing, something to be thankful for.

People brought him food and, through the efforts of his emergency guardian, all of the utility companies turned on services to his home. The Mosholders paid the bank $6,000 to discontinue the foreclosure proceedings. A trust fund was started and many donated to it. One newspaper story included quotes from a mother commending her young son for handing over his allowance to the fund. Public charities stepped in and provided Bud with free home health care and a hearing aid.

Victor Hugo wrote, "As the purse is emptied, the heart is filled."

Bud would have liked that one because his community gave in the holiday spirit and his situation was no longer desperate.

I eventually located Bob Cote and interviewed him. He insisted that he had only been carrying out Bud's wishes and, coupled with Bud's earlier statements to police that everything was just fine, prosecution under a grand theft statute looked very difficult. That law required the victim's lack of consent.

Now that the exploitation statute had been shot down by the courts, the state refused to prosecute Bob Cote. He walked away. Or rather, he drove away in his Corvette after spending more than $200,000 of Bud's money.

Something good did come out of Bud's case. The public attention that it attracted helped to motivate Florida lawmakers to write a good exploitation law, one of the best in the nation. Monica Hofheinz and representatives from the Attorney General's Office and other government enforcement agencies formed a committee that met regularly for months to prepare the new bill. I was there too and was impressed with the dedication of each person on the committee. No one had any agenda except to write the toughest law to fight exploitation crimes.

Our proposed bill addressed not only those who exploit, but those who "assist" in the exploitaton, including attorneys, notaries and stockbrokers. It prohibited intimidation of the victim and raised the level of exploitation crimes to a first degree felony if enough assets were stolen.

Our bill also recognized the problem of victim disabilities, including short-term memory loss. Criminal investigators could give related testimony of victims' statements without having to be medical experts.

This bill, titled "CS/SB 82," was completed and sponsored for the March 1995 legislation session. It was unanimously passed in both the House and Senate to become law. Today it is Florida Statute 825.103.

Sadly, on June 11, just a couple of months after the bill was passed, Bud Witt died of natural causes. A local newspaper reporter who had followed Bud's plight wrote,

"Bud Witt died Sunday in the tiny apartment that used to be his office, in the building he used to own, next door to the house that he once bought as an investment."

But Bud's ordeal was not in vain. His plight truly had motivated the state legislature to pass a better law to protect the elderly.

So in a way, one could say, "Bud, this bill's for you!" I think that he would have liked that one.

CHAPTER 7

THE KEY ISSUE

August 1994

She lay in bed in the middle of the night watching the phone as it rang again and again. She hated that relentless, incessant ringing, but not as much as the demon on the other side who waited for her to pick up, just one more time.

"I shouldn't let this bother me. This has to stop. I'm 93 years old for God's sakes!" she thought.

She reached out with one trembling hand and brought the receiver to her ear.

"Hello?"

Heavy breathing. Then, "Aaaauughhhh."

Silence.

Then, again from the receiver, she heard, "Aaaaaggghheelllp."

It had begun yet again, those same shrill cries and screams, sounding like someone in terrible pain. The elderly woman, Ina Weiner, repeated the same question that she had asked the other times.

"Who is this? Please."

Heavy breathing.

"Please leave me alone!"

"Aaauuuggghhhh. Aaaaagggghhhhhhhh."

"Why do you keep taunting me like this? Leave me alone!"

She hung up the phone and unplugged the chord from the wall, though she hated to do that. What if that demon came to her instead?

When Ina woke up the next morning, she washed, made her morning coffee, turned the ringer on the kitchen phone back on and returned to the bedroom to plug that phone back into the wall. It had become a routine during the past week.

But no sooner had she plugged the phone back in than it started ringing again. She waited for a few rings and then picked it up.

"Hello?"

"Hello Ina, how are you this morning? This is Sharon."

Ina recognized the voice and Caribbean accent before the caller even said her name. Truth was that Ina expected the call anyway.

"What do you want, Sharon?"

"Listen, I need more money, Ina."

"But I've already given you plenty of money. Why don't you leave me alone?"

"Ina, I still have the key to the garage. Don't make me use it."

Ina paused and sighed.

"How much do you want, Sharon?"

"I'll tell you what Ina, give me another $500, okay?"

"Will you leave me alone after that?"

"Ina, I promise you I'll leave you alone. I'll come by this afternoon to give you the key, you give me the money and everything will be fine, okay?"

Ina agreed and Sharon Wilcox, her former caretaker, came to the house that afternoon. Ina gave her a $500 check and Sharon gave Ina the garage key.

In two weeks, this made $2,000 that Ina had paid for her own house keys.

Now maybe Sharon would leave her alone and wouldn't "use the keys," as threatened. Maybe the calls would stop. Maybe Ina could have some peace. After all, a 93-year-old shouldn't have to go through this.

Extortion is a cruel thing. One person maliciously threatens another to force the victim to do something against his or her will, usually for some type of financial gain. It's about oppression for profit. It can also be a form of elderly exploitation when the victim and culprit are brought together initially by the victim's disability.

In Ina's case, the disability was a broken wrist.

Ina was an independent and mentally sharp woman in good physical condition, but she had snapped her wrist. Showering and cooking meals one-handed would be difficult for a person of any age, so Ina hired a daytime helper during her recovery at home. Sharon Wilcox, a 38-year-old home health aide, was the new assistant.

After three months, Ina's wrist had healed and she no longer needed assistance. There wasn't any problem with the care that Wilcox provided, but Ina was an independent woman who enjoyed her privacy.

But when she gave Wilcox the news and two weeks severance pay, the caretaker became belligerent and angry. Before leaving Ina's home she demanded, and received, another $500. Ina just wanted to get her out of the house.

Several hours after Wilcox left the house, she called Ina on the phone and said that she still had the front door key. She demanded another $500 and Ina paid her. Wilcox planned no end to this extortion and the nighttime calls began with the eerie screams, cries and animal noises followed by calls the following mornings for yet more money.

During this week of haunting calls and extortion payments, a neighbor noticed that Ina's behavior had changed. The sweet, old woman had stopped going on morning walks, tinkering in her yard and picking up the daily newspaper from the driveway. At night, all of Ina's house lights were out, except the bedroom.

So the neighbor prodded Ina for an explanation until she finally confided her predicament. The neighbor persuaded Ina to talk to the police.

Troubled by the apparent extortion of a 93-year-old woman, the police officer who responded to the call decided to phone me directly, asking me to come to the house.

If extortion is about oppression, justice is about fairness. Since Wilcox was using the phone to torment Ina, it only seemed fair to use the phone to help me arrest Wilcox. This could be done by attaching a voice activated recorder to Ina's phone and having the phone company put a trace on her line to verify the location of the incoming calls.

Due to the recent ruling by the Florida Supreme Court, no exploitation statute existed at this time, but I could use other laws against Wilcox such as extortion and grand theft.

Since Ina was clearheaded and chose to prosecute so that, in her own words, she "could get some sleep," we decided to install the recorder and initiate the trace as quickly as possible.

As I set up the recorder, I wrote her a few basic questions to ask such as, "How much do you want?" and "What will you do if I don't pay you?"

She sat on the bed reviewing the questions while I plugged the recorder into the phone with a simple double-jack device. The phone rang almost immediately.

Ina answered and pointed at it while talking. It was Wilcox. I had hooked up the recorder just in time.

The following is a transcript from that call.

"Hello?"

"Hello Ina, listen here, I'm going crazy. I really need a job, I can't find a job."

"Well Sharon, you always told me it would be easy to get one. I'm sorry but I can't do anything more to help you.. I've been stripped of money and I gave you all the money that I have."

"Oh, come on now, Ina, You got money."

"Well, just what is it that you want me to do?"

"All that I want you to do is to give me more money to help me pay some of my bills."

"I can't help you to pay your bills anymore."

Silence.

I was listening to Ina's end of the conversation and now I pointed to the questions that I had written out for her. Poor Ina was doing a good job, but she wasn't an actress and so she read the questions directly from the sheet.

"Tell me how much you want?"

"How much do I want? How much can you afford to give me, Ina?"

"Tell me how much you want?"

There was silence for a few seconds. Wilcox hesitated and then replied,

"I said whatever you can afford to give me, Ina."

Ina became a bit nervous now and read directly from the sheet again.

"How much do you want and…What will you do if I don't pay you?"

"If you don't pay me? What are you trying to get at, Ina? What are you up to?"

Ina's hands were shaking noticeably now.

"I just want to end this thing, the torment that you're putting me through."

"Ina, you know something? I'm not dumb, okay? And you're trying to set me up and that's not gonna work, okay?"

Wilcox hung up.

It looked like this was not going to be the "slam-dunk" case that it first appeared to be. I started to explain this to Ina but then the phone rang again.

It was Wilcox.

"Hello Ina? Listen here, my car is not working so here's what you're gonna do. You can mail me another five hundred dollars, okay? That's the way that we'll do it."

Wilcox took the bait after all. Despite suspecting that she was being set up, greed got the best of her. Now there was certainly enough evidence to justify taking her into custody as quickly as possible.

The rest is "elementary," as Sherlock Holmes would say, and Wilcox was arrested the following day for grand theft. She cried while being handcuffed and delivered to the county jail – proof that, like extortion, justice also can be an oppressive thing.

But the key issue in this case was quick intervention.

What if it hadn't happened that way?

What if Ina's neighbor hadn't cared enough to check up on her or the police hadn't taken quick action? Wouldn't it be reasonable to assume that Wilcox would have continued to torment and extort Ina out of her money, very possibly until she was completely broke like Bud Witt?

Or would Wilcox have "used the keys" at some point? If so, would anyone have ever known?

CHAPTER 8

The Poor Father
Part I

"Not he who has little, but he who wishes for more, is poor."
Lucius Seneca, 65 AD

July 1994

The Everglades House, Point of Americas and the Atlantic Towers are just a few of the pricey, high-rise condominiums located by the Atlantic Ocean on the southeast tip of Fort Lauderdale. As part of the lavish community of Harbor Beach, they are the homes of many well-to-do retirees who moved there decades earlier to enjoy their "golden years."

Saint Sebastian Church is conveniently located nearby. It plays an important role in the community, a source of encouragement and comfort for many of the Catholic retirees, especially those who have lost their spouses.

This case focuses on the people in that affluent community and their relationship with their priest. It illustrates an unusual type of victimization of the lonely and disabled, and reveals that exploitation is not beneath any profession or prevented by any institution.

It was about 9 p.m., a time when most of the elderly residents were settled for the night. Rampersad Goolcharan had just finished making his rounds. He sat down at his post in the front lobby of the Everglades House condominiums and was about to catch up on some reading, but motion caught the corner of his eye. He looked back to see a tall, dark figure stepping quietly out the side service doors. Normally the security guard would have been alarmed, but he recognized the man's white hair and collar over the black outfit, the garb of the local priest. "Probably on his rounds too," Rampersad thought.

The priest was a broad-shouldered man in his mid-sixties who usually was dressed in a worn, faded black shirt and pants. He looked more like a classic "poor-priest-begging-donations" than the spiritual leader of a very wealthy parish. He carried himself in a dignified and reverent manner, though, and was known as a well-spoken man who could captivate his audience during Sunday sermons.

Rampersad could appreciate the priest's devotion, but wished that the good father would use the front doors and sign into the visitors logbook like everyone else. Rules are rules after all and sign-ins made his job that much easier. But he dismissed the incident and relaxed now because not much ever happened in the Everglades House.

Or so it seemed.

Summer is a time when many Floridians become disenchanted with the climate and talk of moving to a "better place" that offers four seasons and friendlier neighbors. The snowbirds go home and traffic isn't as congested, but daily temperatures in the 90s coupled with stifling humidity generally make the locals irritable.

It was a hot July day when Bill Schneider, the building manager of the Everglades House, contacted me at the Fort Lauderdale Police Department's Fraud Unit. He reported that an elderly resident was being ripped off by her caretaker. The complaint appeared routine.

The victim, Bernedice McCurdy, was 86-years-old and her mental health had deteriorated over the past few years. Her appearance also was bad now, with unbrushed hair and a torn dress becoming common in recent months. She gave off a strong odor and would go down to the front office several times a day to ask Bill the same question or tell the same story.

The caretaker, 30-year-old Rhonda Hamilton, was going to the victim's condominium several times a day but staying for very short periods of time – about 20 minutes per visit. This made Bill suspicious. On the same day he called me, Bill tried to stop Hamilton when she was leaving, but she ran to her car and sped away. While fleeing, the caretaker had dropped three of Bernedice's checks to the ground and Bill recovered them. Each check was made out to Hamilton for $350, with the same date and the same notation: "Weeks salary."

It sounded like a classic exploitation case where the caretaker takes advantage of the victim's short-term memory loss by requesting the same payment repeatedly. So I served a subpoena on Hamilton's checking account to see if the damage was extensive. Unfortunately it was.

For months, Hamilton had asked the victim for grocery money or her weekly paycheck on a daily basis, sometimes half-a-dozen times a day. The victim had written over 220 checks in small amounts ranging between $50 to $300, totaling $53,000 over several months. Almost all of the checks had notations on them such as "groceries" or "weekly salary."

The evidence against Hamilton was strong. The excessive number of checks and the large amount stolen offered especially damning evidence so I decided to move quickly to get the victim's statement proving Bernedice's lack of capacity.

It was a hot day, probably in the mid-90s, when I left the police station for Bernedice's condo. Once there, I had to take an elevator from the lobby to the eighth floor, where an outdoor catwalk led to her front door. The view of the Atlantic Ocean was beautiful, but the heat and humidity made the trip a sweaty one and my new white dress-shirt was already wet with perspiration. I knocked but had to repeatedly explain to her through the closed door that I was a detective. Finally, she let me in.

When I stepped inside there was no relief from the heat. There was a strong odor and it was dark. Bernedice explained that she liked the lights turned off and thermostat set on high to save on electric. She also kept her shades down because she believed that the sun would ruin her furniture.

When we entered her living room, I saw that she had been doing paperwork of some kind on her coffee table, which sat between two couches. Piles of opened and unopened letters were stacked high on the table, along with her checkbook ledger and folders of financial documents.

She was very hospitable at first, offering me a glass of water, which I accepted. But her memory loss became evident when she returned three times to ask me why she had gone to the kitchen. While she was away, I sat down on the couch by the coffee table and noticed a stub in the checkbook ledger from the prior year that was made out to a "Father Hudak" for $2,500. There was a notation on it, "Trip to Rome." I asked Bernedice about this and she explained that the priest had wanted to go to Rome to see the pope, but priests are poor and he couldn't afford it. So she had helped to pay his way. I wondered why a priest would take such a gift from a woman who must have been in this same mental condition at the time the check was written. But I decided to let that sleeping dog lie, at least for the moment.

After Bernedice at last brought me the water and sat down, we talked about the caretaker. She explained how Rhonda Hamilton would spend the day cleaning her home for 75 cents an hour and on occasion even go out to buy some groceries.

I felt sad that yet another exploitation victim was describing a congenial relationship with a caretaker who was actually a predator. The pay was not 75 cents an hour, Rhonda was not spending the day there and the motive was not care, but greed.

After we talked for a few minutes, I placed my tape recorder on the coffee table and explained that I was going to do a quick interview. She didn't really agree or disagree to it, but only stared at me sternly. Her demeanor was changing and I later wished that I had paid more attention to that before pushing the record button.

"Bernedice, as I told you, I'm a police officer and it's my job to make sure that your finances are safe and no one is taking advantage of you. Do you understand that?"

"My finances are absolutely fine. Do you know who takes care of them?"

"No, who?"

"The father at the church."

She threw me off with this information. This was the first that I had heard of it.

"Could you tell me the father's name and the church?"

"Ahhh – well, I wish you wouldn't have asked me that, because I really can't remember at the moment. But wait -- it's Saint Sebastian's. It's in renovation now and they're going to rebuild the whole church. I'm going to the parish."

I recalled the name of the priest mentioned in her checkbook ledger.

"Father Hudak, is it Father Hudak that helps you with your finances?"

She laughed, "Why of course not. He's busy taking care of his parishioners."

I was getting a little frustrated now, sweaty and uncomfortable in the heat of her condo, so I moved on quickly to the issue of the caretaker.

"Okay, let's just talk about your finances for a moment. Do you know how much money in checks you've written and signed in just the past few months?"

"Absolutely, and it's none of your business. If I wrote $500,000 in checks it's none of your business."

She was scowling at me, obviously not liking any talk about her finances. This appeared to be her sore spot. I could have changed the subject for a while, but I really wanted to leave her home as soon as possible, so I pressed on.

"Okay well, do you know Rhonda Hamilton?"

"Yes, she was here today. I gave her some money and she's out buying me groceries right now."

"Great, how much did you give her?"

She leaned forward towards me and looked directly into my eyes.

"I don't think that's any of your business. If I gave her a million dollars that's none of your business."

"Well, I'm a little concerned because it looks like you wrote Rhonda checks for over $53,000 during the past couple of months."

That seemed to push her over the edge.

"No! Where did you get that figure? I couldn't have written them if I wanted to because I don't have that much money."

She leaned toward me further.

"And I still can't understand why you're here monkeying around in my business."

I tried to calm her down, but it was too late.

"Bernedice, please calm down. I'm not trying to upset you but I'm sure about this, and …"

"No, I haven't done anything like that and now you can get moving!"

I really should have seen it coming. Her aggressive posture and demeanor sent up warning flags, but I ignored them.

She reached down, picked up the tape recorder and threw it into my face. I jumped back to protect myself, but it was too late. Blood trickled down from my cheek onto my white shirt as I blurted out profanities.

I put one hand to my face and extended the other outward against another assault, but rather than attacking me again, Bernedice was already sitting back calmly in her seat. She looked at me as if nothing had happened. I'm not sure she even realized the seriousness of what she had done and I didn't really care right then.

At that point, I just wanted to get the hell out of there. And I did. Instantly.

I closed the door and walked back down the catwalk towards the elevator and my once-clean, new white shirt was now soaked with sweat and spattered with blood. It was just a small cut on my left cheek that would mend quickly enough, quicker than my pride, but I dreaded the ribbing I would take back at the office. Here I was, a big strong cop looking like …well, like I had just been beaten up – by a little old lady! This just wasn't right.

Adult Protective Services was already beginning emergency guardianship proceedings for Bernedice. There appeared to be no reason for me to return and I decided that it would take an act of God to get me there.

But just a week later, I received a phone call from Bill Schneider, the building manager. He wanted me to come back for an unusual reason.

"Joe, I know how busy you are with the caretaker and your other cases and I really hate to do this to you, but I think that the local priest is also taking advantage of Bernedice."

A social worker evaluating Bernedice for the guardianship hearing had revealed to him some shocking information that came from the elderly woman.

Bernedice had confided to the social worker that, just the evening before, Father Hudak had visited her condo and told her to retrieve her will from a bank safe deposit box. The priest had said Bernedice should bring the document to him.

Bill had spotted Bernedice when she was leaving the building and asked where she was going. To get her will, she had answered. He also had called Rampersad, the evening security guard, who confirmed seeing the priest slip out the service doors at about 9 p.m. the previous night – and as usual the father hadn't signed in.

I agreed that it all sounded suspicious, but pointed out that it wasn't fair to jump to conclusions based on the words of a mentally incapacitated woman. We decided that it would be best to just keep our eyes open for the time being.

Despite my reply to Bill, though, I had a nagging feeling.

I could understand a different type of situation, where a priest was so busy dealing with parishioners that he hadn't noticed one elderly church member's slightly diminished mental capacity. But in this instance, Bernedicc's appearance and behavior broadcast pretty clearly that she was mentally disabled. One would have expected the father to seek ways to alleviate the woman's obvious self-neglect, especially after he was inside her home. Instead, his name was written on her check stub.

And that's when it struck me – I remembered Bernedice's opening line in her statement to me.

"My finances are absolutely fine. Do you know who takes care of them?"

I decided to make a taped call to Father Hudak. Either he would have simple answers to my questions and the matter would be finished or he would be deceptive and I would have evidence. I truly expected a simple explanation.

The date of this call was August 11, 1994 and the following are excerpts from that transcript.

"Hi Father, this is Detective Roubicek."

"What did I do wrong now?"

I laughed. "How are you today sir? Do you know a Mrs. McCurdy?"

"Uh yeah, we have her name here at the church."

"Did you see her today or yesterday?"

"She called me on the phone. I haven't seen her today, no. Something wrong?"

I explained the problem with the caretaker and told him about the emergency guardianship proceedings. He sympathized.

"That's unfortunate. I understand that happens a lot with these older people."

"Yes it does. Father, I know that Bernedice gets confused, but the reason that I'm calling you is because she said that you told her to get her will and bring it to you over at the church."

"Oh my heavens! You see, I go over there to give people spiritual help. That's what I'm here for. I don't have anything to do with her finances whatsoever. If she gave me a million dollars I wouldn't take it because it wouldn't be proper. It should go through the Archbishop or someone like that."

"Good enough, Father. If anything related should happen, I would appreciate it if you would call me."

"Oh yes! And your name is Joe? A captain?"

"No, just a detective. So Father, are you sure that you haven't discussed her will with her at all?"

"No, I can't imagine what she's up to. I have seen her in the little chapel during Mass, but I didn't even speak to her. Are you of Polish background, Joe?"

"I sure am."

"Well, so am I. Where are you from?"

Apparently he wanted to get to know me too. I had no problems with answering a few of his personal questions and after we exchanged more pleasantries, our call ended on an amiable note.

After I hung up, my first thought was that the priest wasn't just deceptive – he was damn good at it. I had caught him by surprise, yet he had remained calm but evasive.

Unless someone had impersonated Father Hudak, or the security guard was terribly mistaken, the priest was lying.

So I decided to investigate this man of God, but with reluctance. Not because I was concerned about who he was, but because of who I am.

I was once a poor altar boy, raised along with seven brothers and sisters by a school-teaching, single mother who practically lived in the Catholic Church when she wasn't working. Priests were our moral icons of goodness, they weren't bad guys.

I investigated bad guys.

Still, I began the formal investigation and almost immediately the incriminating, disturbing facts came at me as swiftly as that tape recorder thrown by Bernedice.

I made that first, taped phone call to Father Hudak on August 11th. What I didn't know was that on the following day, Bernedices' stockbroker received a letter from her dated August 10th requesting that $10,100 be gifted to Father Hudak from her brokerage account. The priest also visited her broker that same week, claiming that he stopped by to say hello and get acquainted. Then on August 15th, just four days after my call to the priest, Bernedice called her broker and cancelled the written gift request.

Bernedice was incapable of writing that gift letter, so I assumed that Father Hudak was behind it and it appeared that he was backing down because of my call.

He wasn't. He was just trying a different approach.

On September 7, I received an urgent phone call from Bill Schneider at the Everglades House. He said that Father Hudak had been over to see Bernedice twice the day before, once in the afternoon and again at night. The security guard, Rampersad, made sure that the priest signed the visitors log on both occasions. Bill said that Bernedice was going back to the bank to empty her safe deposit box because Father Hudak had instructed her to bring him the contents for safekeeping.

I later went to the bank and confirmed with the head teller that Bernedice had indeed accessed her safe deposit box that morning. But the teller also gave me a new, surprising piece of information. On the prior day, the day of the priest's visits to Bernedice, Father Hudak had attempted to cash one of Bernedice's checks for $350 at that same branch, but there were insufficient funds in her account and the check was returned to him. The teller was sure of the amount and the fact that the check was made out specifically to "Cyril Hudak."

I wondered why the priest would do such a bold thing when he knew that I could find out. At the least his good reputation would be threatened, or worse, he could be charged criminally. These were unusual actions for such an intelligent man with so much to lose.

Unless, of course, he thought that he was above the law.

I made another taped phone call to the priest that same day, but changed my approach. Instead of telling him upfront that I was calling about the $350 check, I emphasized that anyone who took money from Bernedice was committing a crime due to her lack of capacity. The purpose of the call was to make the case stronger by taking away his defense that he "didn't know." It was this call that made his intentions clear and identified, at least for me, the type of person that Father Hudak really was.

"Thanks for your time again, Father. As I told you, we are doing a criminal investigation and we're concerned about Bernedice, who is about to be assigned to an emergency guardian. Three doctors have examined her and all of them found her to be mentally incapacitated."

"Oh boy!" he exclaimed. "You know, Joe, I was reading an article in the *Miami Herald* a week or two ago about guardians and how they're stripping the old people of their estates."

"Really, Father?"

"Well, they take advantage of all these old people once they become their guardians. I really think that's kind of sad. Bernedice might not be any better off with a guardian than she is with these girls because the guardians can steal the money just as easily."

And how about priests, Father? I wanted to say it, but didn't.

"Well, Father, I guess that you just have to try to find the lesser of two evils and we can only try, right?"

"Yes. By the way Joe, will the guardian have full control over everything that she spends?"

"Yes. Full control over everything, Father."

"So she has to ask the guardian, then, when she wants money and so forth?"

"Yes, that's right. Father, have you seen her at church or have you been to her place at all recently?"

"I think that it was at the 11 o'clock Mass last Sunday. She says hello when she's leaving with all the people."

"Have you been to her place recently?"

I wanted to see if he would admit being there the prior day.

"Let's see -- I'm checking my calendar. I would have been there to give her communion on the first Friday. That would have been a week ago today."

"A week? Okay. Thank you for your time today, Father."

"Oh, thank you, Joe. Bye."

This time the priest had sounded disappointed. Bernedice's assets were about to be legally tied up by a guardianship.

I served a subpoena on Bernedice's bank for the security video that showed Father Hudak attempting to cash her check. I also obtained records of the priest's checking account, which happened to be with the same bank. The result was stunning.

In that one account, this local Catholic priest had $112,000. Over the prior year, he had moved more than $225,000 through this same account. Most of the larger checks going through were from brokerage accounts or the sale of properties.

A background check on Father Hudak revealed that he was also a licensed real estate agent. He owned more than six properties in Florida and one address in particular stood out: 2200 South Ocean Lane, #2309, a high-priced condo on the 23rd floor of the Point Of Americas II. It appeared that the good father was a millionaire.

Was it an inheritance or a gift? That was the question. When interviewed, the building manager of Point Of Americas told me that an elderly woman named Dorothy Flynn owned that condo through the 1980s. She had died and Father Hudak took ownership. I also interviewed the occupant of the condo, a renter paying $2,000 a month to the priest. That's $24,000 a year in rental income.

With some investigative effort, I eventually was able to locate the executor of Dorothy Flynn's estate and two attorneys who were directly familiar with the matter. The three of them told me that Father Hudak and Dorothy Flynn had a private relationship. As part of that relationship, Flynn would buy properties and Hudak would manage them. Eventually Flynn became terminally ill, but she had already signed a will making the priest beneficiary to half of her properties. The Point of Americas condo was one of these.

The legal problems with Father Hudak were not over the condo, but an additional $200,000 in stocks that the priest had Flynn sign over while in her deathbed. The executor and attorneys representing Flynn's estate went after the priest in probate court for undue influence. After threatening to drag the issue before the Archdiocese and media, they got him to sign the stocks back over to the estate. The matter was then considered closed.

I would have thought that this experience might have tempered Hudak's greedy behavior. Clearly, it hadn't.

On September 19, my secretary told me that Father Hudak was on the phone. He was irate and got right to the point.

"Joe, you've called me a number of times and now I receive notice from the bank that you have served papers on my account. Why are you determined to involve me in some type of criminal investigation?"

"Well Father, for a start I have you visiting Bernedice on the 6th and then you're at the bank attempting to cash her $350 check that same day. You're on the bank's video, Father. I call you on the following day and you deny seeing her or taking her money."

"I was just trying to see if there was any money in her account so that we could pass through other checks that she had written to the parish. I had absolutely no intention of, and never will, accept any money from her. My records and my bank statements are nobody else's God damned business but my own!"

"Father, you have a lot of money in your accounts and my concern is ..."

"Where did I get it, or who did I steal it from? Bernedice has been the last thing on my mind for any kind of gift. Just between you and me, Joe, she had been a very good friend of a priest that was here, a Monsignor. I heard that she was buying him round trip tickets to Ireland and she'd take him to dinners and buy him gifts. I said to all the people around here, 'If Bernedice ever sends me any gifts, you send them right back.'"

"Okay, Father. Give me time to look at everything rather than just talk about it over the phone, and I'll get back to you."

"Joe, priests are very vulnerable people. If some crazy lady should go to the *Sun-Sentinel* or *Miami Herald* and give them a bum story, there's no way we could overcome it. Look what happened to Cardinal Bernadine in Chicago."

"I understand, Father"

"Thank you, Joe."

The time had come to sit down with the prosecutor to determine what actions, if any, would be taken against the priest. At this point in the game, Father Hudak knew that a significant investigation was under way and that there was evidence against him.

Unfortunately, this was in November 1994. Bud Witt's exploitation was about to hit the newspapers and there was no exploitation statute to protect him – or Bernedice. The prosecutor's hands were pretty much tied, though he still filed grand theft charges against exploiters whenever possible.

After reviewing the case, the prosecutor said that he would not file charges against the priest for attempting to obtain the $10,100 gift or the will. There was no evidence that the priest possessed either one and the main witness was the mentally incapacitated victim. A trial would have pitted the word of a prominent priest against the testimony of an elderly woman who couldn't tell a jury what year it was.

But the prosecutor did agree to file a grand theft charge against the priest for attempting to cash the $350 check. This situation was different because the case was not based on the victim's memory but on statements provided by the bank's head teller. That evidence was supported by the security video, the father's own taped admission of possessing the check and his taped denial of visiting Bernedice on that same day. The prosecutor now only needed a sworn statement from the head teller so that he could file the charge.

It appeared that Father Hudak soon would go to jail.

The following day, I took the bank teller's statement and everything was going fine until we got to the amount of the check.

"On September 7th did Father Hudak present you with a check to be cashed?"

"Yes, he did."

"Was the check made out to Cyril Hudak, or Saint Sebastian Church?"

"Cyril Hudak. It had to be. We could not have cashed a check for the church, which is a business account. It was definitely made out to him."

"Okay, can you tell me how much the check was for?"

"Ummm. I'm not sure now. That was weeks ago and we don't have the check to refresh my memory. How much did I tell you back then? Was it $350?"

"Yes, you specifically told me that it was for $350. You remember that, right?"

"Yes, if you say so, then it was. I'm sorry, but I've cashed a lot of checks since then and I can't remember. Normally I have a copy of the check sitting in front of me when I give these statements. You really should have taken my statement weeks ago when you were here."

She was right, I should have.

My heart sank because I knew that the priest was about to get out of a felony charge. At that time in Florida, grand theft charges were based on taking $300 or more and I could no longer prove the actual amount.

Now the priest only faced a misdemeanor charge of petty theft. If he were arrested, his bond would be $25 and he would bond out within the hour. What were the odds, I wondered, that the prosecutor would charge a prominent priest for the "attempted" petty theft of an unknown amount of money from a mentally incapacitated old lady?

When I asked him, he smiled and said, "Joe, I'm not stupid."

It looked like Father Hudak was a free man.

****

Part II

December 1994

Just when it appeared that the time had come to close the case against Father Hudak, an anonymous caller suddenly led me to a new victim.

I listened to a remarkable story about an elderly widow who had given everything that she had to Father Hudak and after he cast her aside, she attempted suicide.

Her name was Dorothy Penta and she had once lived in the Atlantic Towers, another high-rise near the Everglades House. Dorothy was mentally alert but suffered back problems that kept her mostly confined to her home. The tipster gave me the phone number for her sister, Marjorie, of Hickory, North Carolina. I was told Marjorie could provide more details.

When I called, Marjorie told me that Dorothy now was living on welfare in a nearby nursing home and doing much better since the ordeal of two years prior. Then she told me a story remarkable enough that I asked her to retell it in a formal statement during the same interview. This was her account of the events.

"Well, Dorothy called me from the hospital. She was there because she had attempted suicide with an overdose of pills. She refused to give me the details but said that she was in dire trouble. So I made immediate arrangements and flew down to Fort Lauderdale the next morning.

"When I picked her up at the hospital she told me that she was broke. I asked her how this could have happened and she just kept saying that she didn't know. So I wrote her a check for $1,000 to help cover expenses for the week and stayed with her for a couple of days until things calmed down.

"While I was going through her things, I realized that her diamond engagement ring was missing. I said, 'Dorothy, your ring is missing,' and she said, 'Well, Father Hudak is taking care of it for me.' I had always suspected that she was giving that priest money, but I never knew how much. She liked to keep her financial affairs to herself.

"Later on that day, I called Father Hudak at the rectory and said that I was coming over to get the ring and he said fine. When we met, he gave it to me and I asked him if he knew that Dorothy was broke and destitute. He just looked at me and said, 'Yes.' I told him that I knew that she had been giving him money and that it would be the Christian thing for him to at least return some of it to her. He said, 'I don't intend to give her anything and it's your word against mine that I've gotten any money from her at all.' Well, I told him to think it over and that I'd be around for a couple of days, but I never heard from him again."

"Did you complain to the Archdiocese?"

"No, I spoke to my attorney who said that the monies from Dorothy were gifts and if I made any trouble, the priest could go after me for slander. So I didn't."

"What did Dorothy say about giving money to Father Hudak?"

"Before this she never said much, maybe a vague comment about giving him money on occasion, but she was mostly secretive about it. I was shocked to hear that she didn't have any left, because I thought that she had about $500,000 when her husband died three years earlier. Since her suicide attempt, I've obtained copies of about a dozen cashier's checks for over $20,000 that she had given to the priest. They were made out to cash and endorsed by 'Cyril Hudak' on the back. I'll be happy to send them to you if you'd like."

An investigation with a mentally alert victim, witnesses and physical evidence right from the start sounded too good to be true. If her information proved correct, I would have a strong criminal case this time. But was Dorothy really still that sharp and would she prosecute?

Marjorie gave me her phone number at the retirement home. I called immediately and took her first statement by phone.

"Dorothy, you know Father Cyril Hudak?"

"Oh, I sure do, that great big gigolo!"

"Between 1990 and 1992, you had given the Father some money, correct?"

"It actually started before then. My husband died six years ago, so it was right after he died that it started with Father. He always said that he had no money at all and oh, if you could have seen the clothes that he wore."

"Do you remember how much money you gave the father over the years?"

"For starters I gave him $4,000 to put down on a car and then $400 per month so that he could make the car payments. He bought a convertible, a white one."

"Did you give him the money because he told you that he was poor?"

"Yes. He said that he only got $85 a month from the church."

"And did you believe him when he told you that he was poor?"

"I did. I bought his clothes, his shoes, gave him money for food and everything. Then he took trips to visit his brothers and sisters, or other priests."

"Dorothy, your sister is sending me about $20,000 in checks that you gave him."

"Oh, I gave him a lot more than that. Sometimes I would give him $10,000 at a time for this and that, but when I came to him for money, and I only asked him for $2,000, he said that he didn't have a dime and would have to sell his car to get it for me."

"So you said that you gave him $10,000 at a time. How did you give it to him?"

"Well, it was some type of a cashier's check. He said that he would rather have it that way."

"Can you tell me specifically what he told you in reference to his being poor?"

"Oh, he said that he had no money and his shoes were all worn out and his house needed repair and he didn't have anything to eat."

"Did he ever promise to pay you back any of the money?"

"No, it was always a gift."

"About how much of it do you think you gave to him?"

"At least a hundred thousand."

"A hundred thousand? You're kidding! Did you ever give him jewelry?"

"Yes, my diamond engagement ring. He said that I shouldn't keep anything valuable in the house and I should give it to him to hold for safekeeping."

"Has he ever given you any money back whatsoever?"

"Not a dime. I asked him again for $2,000 after I – well, you know, after I ended up out here, but he never sent it."

"Dorothy, isn't it possible that you just assumed that he was poor?"

"No. He specifically said that he didn't have any money. He said that he didn't know what he was going to do."

"What if Father Hudak was charged criminally for doing this to you, would you want to prosecute him?"

"Oh yes, I would."

During the time when Father Hudak refused to give his former benefactor any money, he was swimming in dough. He simply could have given her one month's rent payment of $2,000 from his inherited condo. Even after Dorothy's suicide attempt, though, he wouldn't give her a cent and wouldn't even see her, yet made plenty of time for Bernedice and other gift givers.

I knew, of course, that there was a stark contrast between Father Hudak and the countless other priests who gave portions of their own meager salaries to the poor in their parishes. Some priests even relied on financial gifts that they received in a legitimate manner to supplement their salaries and retirement.

To learn how gift giving was regulated in the Catholic Church, I requested a meeting with the Archdiocese of Miami. The meeting was held at the Archdiocese headquarters with the Moderator Of The Curia and the Archdiocese Financial Administrator. They explained that, contrary to popular belief, many priests were not "order priests" and had not taken any vow of poverty. Father Hudak was not an order priest and could live any way he liked.

At the time, Catholic priests were treated much like independent contractors by the Archdiocese. They received 1099 tax forms and paid their own Social Security taxes on their $14,000 annual salary. The church usually helped retired priests in need, but there was no legal obligation or any guarantee of this assistance.

I found it difficult to imagine anyone saving for retirement off a $14,000 salary.

Financial support for the fathers through gifts from parishioners made sense, but this investigation was not about honest priests getting legitimate gifts. It was about one dishonest priest getting gifts through exploitation.

The Archdiocese had no regulations about gift taking by its priests. When a priest performed services like a wedding, funeral, or baptism, the money donated for the service was called a "stole fee." The priest would get a small percentage of the stole fee and the remainder went to the church. Priests were required to report and keep an annual accounting of stole fees. But if someone gave money to a priest and specifically told him it was a gift for him, the father was not required to report it in any way. (It should be noted that as a result of our criminal investigation, the Archdiocese said it planned to change policy to require the reporting of gifts by priests.) The Moderator Of The Curia promised confidentiality and assured me that the Archdiocese would cooperate in every way with the investigation. He gave me the phone number directly to his secretary if I should need anything and the meeting ended.

Now I decided that it would be a good a time to attempt an in-person interview with Father Hudak. He still believed that I was investigating his dealings with Bernedice, not Dorothy, and I could use that to my advantage. We agreed to meet at the church the following morning.

On my arrival, the priest shook my hand and welcomed me, but he looked stern and sounded abrupt. The church was under renovation and he had already set up folding chairs by the altar where construction was underway. No one else was around.

I began the interview by covering old ground, asking about his attempt to cash Bernedice's check, but he became irate and interrupted me.

Father Hudak leaned toward me and said, "Detective, I am disgusted at the thought of a Roman Catholic priest being under criminal investigation. And I am especially disgusted by the fact that it is being done by you, a Catholic!"

This reminded me of my Catholic elementary school days when the sisters admonished me for putting tacks on their seats or shooting spitballs at classmates. His effort to intimidate with guilt was obvious, but didn't work. I ignored him and moved on to the next question.

"Father, I see that you own a beautiful condo at the Point Of Americas and you inherited it from a woman named Flynn."

He interrupted me again and gave what sounded more like a prepared statement than a genuine response.

"There has been a meeting between a group of priests and a bishop and it was unanimously agreed by those present that priests are unjustly being accused of doing something wrong by taking gifts. Therefore, for their sake, for the sake of all priests and to help defend them, I will not answer any questions that are not directly related to Bernedice."

What a guy. The meeting ended shortly after that.

Things quieted down through January 1995 and I appreciated that because this gave me time to do an accounting of all the cashier's checks and personal checks Dorothy had written to the priest. In the end, I had actual check copies totaling just over $42,000. Dorothy probably had given the father $100,000 including the cash gifts that he requested, but the bottom line was that the cash gifts couldn't be proven. I wasn't too concerned though, because the priest was still looking at a second-degree grand theft charge and that was a far cry from a misdemeanor.

While searching through Father Hudak's account for Dorothy's checks, I also found many others in smaller amounts that were given as gifts by various parishioners for his trip to Rome. I contacted a dozen of these people to see if he had represented himself as poor, or if they just had assumed this.

It turned out that they had merely made an assumption of poverty. All except one elderly woman.

Her first name was Tyree and she had written the priest a check for $100 with the notation "A Wonderful Sabbatical" written across the bottom. Tyree said that she gave him the money because he specifically told her that he was poor and couldn't afford the trip. But she was also very angry with me.

The priest had visited her bedridden husband three times a week before he died, Tyree explained. She said that Father Hudak was a wonderful man with four brothers who were priests and two sisters who were nuns. He had given Mass in the Vatican with the Pope present and he even showed her the pictures to prove it. He was a holy man, a direct representative of God, and I was wrong to investigate him.

Tyree sent me on my way with my tail between my legs and I wondered how many parishioners would feel the same way when all was said and done.

By February 1995, I was scheduled to fly to North Carolina for a final videotaped interview with Dorothy. The prosecutor decided that this would be the last item needed to file the second-degree felony charge against Father Hudak.

Things were still quiet in Saint Sebastian's parish and I just required a little more time before I could actually arrest the priest and finally put a stop to his nighttime visits. Any other person would have been arrested by now, I thought, but it was wise to prepare the strongest case in advance. That certainly was the prosecutor's intent.

On February 10, I left on a 7 a.m. flight. I was scheduled to interview Dorothy at 11 that morning at the retirement home, then her personal physician in his office at 1, and finally her sister at 3, before catching a 7 p.m. flight back to Fort Lauderdale. It was going to be a long day, but the investigation was a half-year old and I was just glad to be finally wrapping it up.

Hickory was one beautiful North Carolina town, with rolling hills blanketed in snow. The crisp air had the smell of oak from burning fireplaces and the people were very friendly. No one was in a rush in Hickory.

The retirement home was also impressive, with a friendly staff and quaint atmosphere. Dorothy was in her room, sitting in a lounge chair, wearing a dress and looking like she was ready to go out for dinner or maybe a show. She was 86-years-old at the time.

After the stenographer set up the video camera and microphone, I began taking her statement.

Reviewing the cashier's checks with Dorothy for the camera, I commented that it would be difficult for her to recall all of them, and she replied, "No, no, it's not. I've got a bad back, but dammit I've got a good head. I can remember things, detective."

This was going to be fun.

She gave details about the special attentions that Father Hudak had shown her. He would always come to her home to give her communion and call her on Saturday afternoons to make sure that she would be attending the evening Mass. That weekly outing was important to her, one of Dorothy's few excursions away from home. She would sit in the front pew and he would always give her communion first.

The priest had told her that he was a poor man but he had lied, she said now. The last person that she expected to deceive her, Dorothy said, had told her nothing but lies.

I ended the statement by asking Dorothy two things: How did she perceive priests in general and how did she feel about prosecuting this priest?

Her response was certain and to the point.

"Priests are the most wonderful people in the world and the most holy people that I know. And as for prosecuting Father Hudak? It's the only thing left in my life that I want to do before I die."

When the statement ended, I was certain that the priest would be in jail within a week.

This was Friday and by Monday morning I was standing at the prosecutor's desk with a completed arrest affidavit in hand. I had written up a charge of second-degree grand theft against Father Hudak for falsely portraying himself as poor to Dorothy Penta to obtain more than $42,000.

This time our victim was alert, wanted to prosecute and said that she would not have given the money to him without his false statements. Dorothy was also willing to testify against Father Hudak in a court of law. Her tragic story of financial crises, a suicide attempt and life on welfare in a retirement home would be devastating to the priest's defense. None of his parishioners would ever again think he was poor and so the threat of future problems would no longer exist.

There would finally be a happy ending to a long investigation. Amen to that.

I waited in the prosecutor's office as he discussed the arrest one last time with his bosses in the administrative division. After all, arresting a prominent priest from one of the most affluent communities in the city was nothing to take lightly.

An hour passed before he returned. He said that there was a "problem." I couldn't believe it – a problem in the final hour, just as with Bernedice's case.

So I waited for the word "but" to come out in the explanation. It always did. "A crime was committed, but …" "We have plenty of evidence, but …"

Dorothy's mental sharpness seemed a Godsend. It would make her an excellent witness. "But" …could a person properly be charged with theft for taking a gift from another competent person? Even if he lied to get it? Dorothy's mental capacity suddenly looked like a double-edged sword.

The prosecutor explained the issue.

"Joe, if a millionaire dressed up like a homeless person to solicit money by the road, could he be charged with theft? I know it's not the same, but my boss is making a good point. This doesn't mean that we're not charging the priest. We're just going to hold off for the moment while we search for relevant prior case law."

When I was 12, I remember fishing with my older brother at our favorite creek, where I reeled in a two-pound pickerel – the biggest fresh water fish caught in my life. When you're 12, catching a two-pound pickerel is an historic event. Before we left, my brother lifted the fish out of the bucket, took a firm hold and rinsed it off in the creek. I wanted to say, "Couldn't we just get him home and then rinse him off?" But I didn't. Of course the fish escaped my brother's hand and became "the one that got away."

Now I wanted to say to the prosecutor, "Couldn't we just arrest the priest first and then search case law?" I didn't want him to become the one that got away.

I waited for days, which became weeks, until a month had passed and the prosecutor finally called me with news. He said that his office could find no case law in the nation that was related to criminal theft charges for the taking of gifts. Ironically, if Dorothy had lacked full mental capacity things would have been different.

A plea agreement was being negotiated between the priest's attorney and the prosecutor. It wasn't official, but the process had begun that could keep Father Hudak out of jail.

A month later, the State Attorney's Office received the following letter from Dorothy Penta. It would be her final statement in the investigation.

"Per our conversation of April 18,1995, I have made the following decision. Since I was forced to go on welfare because of Reverend Hudak's actions, in lieu of pressing charges against him, I will accept his settlement offer of $70,000 payable immediately.

I also understand that the instant resignation from the Catholic priesthood by Reverend Hudak is an integral part of the agreement.

I hope this action will help prevent him from taking advantage of any other elderly women in the future.

Sincerely,

Dorothy Penta"

That same month, the State Attorney's Office also received a letter signed by the Archbishop of Miami. In it, he accepted Father Hudak's retirement, not resignation, and that retirement would come in the fall rather than immediately. The Archbishop wrote that the retirement was happening for "health reasons," not to avoid criminal charges.

In May, the first Sunday after his case became public, Father Hudak stood before his congregation during Mass and professed his innocence, not knowing that a *Miami Herald* reporter was in the audience. She wrote another article on the case, ending her story with his defense:

"Lack of judgment was used. I know that I committed no crime and in no way did I at any time take advantage of anyone. You must remember that Jesus himself was falsely accused."

The priest retired on schedule and moved into an affluent neighborhood on the Gold Coast of central Florida. A few years later someone said they had seen him on an Alaskan cruise, sitting at a table with an elderly couple, but I haven't heard from him since.

I never heard from Dorothy either, but I hope that $70,000 made the remainder of her life a little easier and I'm glad that she didn't have to go through the stress of a trial.

Rhonda Hamilton was finally charged with second-degree grand theft on March 25, 1996, two years after her theft of over $54,000 from Bernedice.

I walked away from the Father Hudak case a different person, a little more cautious, a little more cynical. Maybe a lot more cynical. I felt as if deception had gotten into everything and realized that the elderly population would always be its victim.

Later this same year I was teaching a course on how to investigate exploitation crimes for the Dade County Criminal Justice Institute. The audience was made up primarily of police officers and adult protective service investigators, with the exception of one particular student. I had just presented a 10-minute video segment from the TV show "A Current Affair" that featured this case when she asked a question that focused on prevention rather than the investigation itself.

"Detective, I understand how the woman with capacity could have been more careful with her money, but could you tell me how the woman without capacity could have avoided this situation?"

"Well, have you heard of the term 'advanced directives'?"

She smiled. "I think so but explain it anyway."

My working with guardianship attorneys in prior investigations has had its advantages and I was about to share their words of wisdom with the class.

"Advanced directives are contracts that designate another person to act on your behalf when you are no longer able to. An example would be a living will, which allows you to designate another person to make medical decisions on your behalf when you no longer can. Obviously this victim could only take preventative action beforehand. She could have hired an elder law attorney to draw up an advanced directive like a trust. Most trusts are called "grantor trusts" and these are contracts between the person setting up the trust and the trustee. If this victim had set up a trust, then after she lost capacity the management of her assets would have fallen into the hands of whoever she chose to be her trustee. Another benefit of a trust is that setting up an estate is often no longer necessary."

While I was answering this "student" she appeared to be shaking her head up and down in agreement and I wondered if I was being tested more than questioned. It was break time anyway and I could check the class roster to see who she was.

"Are there any other questions before we take a break?"

"Yes."

It was her again.

"I believe that during the Current Affair segment they said that the woman had no relatives. So who could she have chosen to be her trustee?"

"Generally, a good choice for trustee would be a corporate fiduciary, like a trust officer at a bank."

"But setting up a trust sounds like it could be costly. What if the woman were not so well off?"

Damn this lady!

"Another reasonable advanced directive is called a durable power of attorney. This is a contract the woman could have used that would simply designate a person of her choice to make financial decisions on her behalf after she lost capacity. I would still recommend using an elder law attorney though. Does anyone else have any questions?"

"One more question. I'm curious, if the woman with capacity; the alert one, gave the priest all her money as a gift, where's the crime?"

At least we were getting back to the criminal investigation.

"Three things are required to prove fraud: material false statements made with intent to deceive, a victim's reliance on these statements and damages. The priest falsely said that he was poor and the victim believed him. She gave him a great deal, went broke and attempted suicide. The prosecutor still considered this to be criminal fraud but he chose to allow the priest to make restitution rather than file charges."

We finally took a break and that relentless student walked up and introduced her self as Doctor Patricia Bloom, the director of the Center on Aging at the University of Miami's School of Medicine. She explained that she was putting together a series of seminars to be conducted throughout Florida for government agencies, foundations and private industry that had an interest in elderly abuse. She asked me to appear as both a lecturer and consultant to their program.

So in the years that followed I found myself working side-by-side with advocates dedicated to better protection of the elderly. It was therapeutic and I became less cynical because I saw that those who exploit the elderly are the minority. The rest of us just have to understand the nature of exploitation crimes so that we can prevent them.

Chapter 9

Mr. Quick, Mrs. Wright And One Bad Lemon
1995-1996

The priest case marked the end of a difficult year of investigations that left me feeling frustrated.

But on July 1, 1995, a new Florida law went into effect. This law introduced phrases like "lacks capacity" and "short-term memory loss" into the statutes. The new language was much more effective and included stiffer penalties that covered almost every type of exploitation scenario. It closed huge loopholes that had protected exploiters living in the Sunshine State.

After that date, prosecutors sometimes still had to rely on the grand theft statute to make their cases stick, but this became the exception rather than the rule.

Now began a consistent string of successful prosecutions and, along with them, public awareness increased significantly. Newspaper articles started to use the word "exploited" rather than "defrauded" far more often. Readers at least had a general understanding that there was a difference.

The following cases represent this new legal crackdown, a welcome shift from the prior "lawless" year. But remember that the law is just a tool and good tools alone do not make a good carpenter.

MR. QUICK

The First Arrest

On July 12, 1995, a 93-year-old German woman named Ottilie was walking up to her car in a shopping center parking lot when a middle-aged man approached her.

He told her that smoke and fire were coming from her car's engine and offered to take a look. Though confused and fearful, she agreed because she thought that she had no choice but to trust him. After a brief inspection under the hood, he convinced her that he could fix the problem, but it was serious and would be very costly. He suggested that they go to her bank for more money. She gave him her car keys and then he literally "took her to the bank."

Once there, he escorted her to a teller window and did all the talking. He told the teller that Ottilie wanted to take out a $4,700 cash advance on her credit card for car repairs.

The teller looked at the tiny, frail woman standing nervously by the man's side and asked her if this was in fact what she wanted.

Ottilie just said "yes." Fortunately, the bank's cameras took their pictures throughout the transaction.

After they left the bank, the man drove them back to the shopping center, got out of the car, and calmly walked away with Ottilie's money. It seemed as if he had done this type of thing before. Ottilie sat there in her car for a while, confused and afraid, and finally asked a passerby to call the police.

When I took this case there was only so much I could do. I got the suspect's picture into the papers, hoping that someone might recognize him. Then I gathered the usual statements from the victim and teller.

In her statement, Ottilie came right out and said that she had lost her memory. She broke down crying and explained that, because of this problem, she couldn't function in her daily living. Sometimes she would wake up in the morning not knowing who or where she was.

Ottilie said that she thought the man had wanted only $47 dollars but couldn't be sure of that either.

Luckily, the bank teller's statement had revealed that the suspect had requested $4,700 for car repairs. Once again, though, I had to listen to a teller tell me that she knew something was wrong during the transaction but thought her hands were legally tied.

Several nights after this incident, a local nightclub manager happened to see the suspect's photo in the local newspaper while the con man was standing right there at the bar. The manager called the police, who responded promptly and took him into custody.

When he arrived at the police station, I was already there waiting.

His name was Tom Quick and he said that he was a Rumanian Gypsy. Quick admitted he was the same person in the bank photo but denied taking any money or telling Ottilie that her car was broken.

The victim was a poor witness because of her memory loss, of course – but the bank teller's memory was just fine. Using the new law, I charged Quick with exploitation.

He was probably the first person in Florida charged under the new law. But the reality is that, if not for an alert nightclub manager, Quick likely would remain today just another nameless face in a bank photo of a crime in progress.

The point being that a good "eye" was needed in addition to the good law and an alert citizen made that difference. Good laws, enforcement and help from the public can solve even the hopeless cases.

MRS. WRIGHT

A Lack Of Safeguards

It would be fair to say that, right up through 1995 in Florida, the guardianship process was frightening.

One could gain immediate and complete legal control over an elderly person and their assets simply by giving false testimony to obtain an emergency guardianship. Throughout this process, the presence and testimony of the elderly person, or "ward," was not required.

Consider the absurdity of all that and the word "frightening" seems too mild.

While a mentally competent senior citizen was sitting at home reading a book or watching TV, someone could be standing before a local probate judge and for malicious reasons, lie to win total authority over that elderly person's life.

There were no safeguards that required monitoring guardians when they put together an accounting of the ward's assets for the court. Unscrupulous guardians simply lied, pocketing jewelry, stock portfolios and bank accounts with little effort.

One guardian, a middle-aged woman named Martha Wright, indirectly helped to change the system for the better by her notorious abuse of it. She was a former maid with no experience in social work, financial management or health care. Yet she convinced judges to give her guardianship over a dozen elderly people and their assets.

Then she systematically wiped them out.

Her worst crimes were committed against a 90-year-old woman named Ethel Hill. Ethel was a retired nurse who had lived a frugal life. Her bank records showed that she rarely wrote a check for over $50 and she had saved well for her later years. She had more than $390,000 in her guardianship account in November 1990, when Wright became her guardian. And these were just the reported assets.

From 1990 through February 1994, Wright cashed for her personal use more than 90 checks totaling in excess of $207,000 from Ethel's account. She forged court orders to get the money from the bank and then forged accounting letters from the bank telling the court that Ethel had $284,000 in her account, when only $28,000 was left.

Soon that money was gone too.

Eventually someone tipped off Adult Protective Services and the media, an investigation began and on June 26 the *Miami Herald* carried a feature article on the "wrongs" of Wright. The very next day she was relieved of all of her guardianships by a probate judge.

For Ethel Hill though, it was too late. She died penniless less than a month later and was buried in a pauper's grave wearing a donated dress because she no longer had one of her own. From the beginning, she had complained to bank tellers and others that Wright was stealing from her, but no one listened. They assumed that she had been justifiably ruled incompetent under the guardianship and couldn't know what she was talking about.

I arrested Wright in September 1995. Finally, she would be held accountable.

It took a full year for investigators to make sense of the paper trail and financial mess that she had left behind. She surrendered to me in the police station lobby with an attorney by her side and, as I placed the handcuffs around her wrists, the attorney told me that Wright had nothing to say. From that point on I was legally bound to respect her right to silence. The irony was that Ethel Hill never had an attorney to protect her right to be heard.

This case and others like it led to intense media coverage and that spotlight helped create a period of significant improvements to the guardianship process throughout Florida. Probate judges required that elderly persons be represented by an attorney, examined by at least one mental health expert, and in attendance at any hearing that determined their fate.

Guardians were required to be bonded to protect wards against fraud or negligence and someone was finally assigned to guard the guardians when they accounted for an elderly person's assets. In Broward County, the Office of the Court Monitor was formed to review and investigate all guardianship applications and accountings, run background checks and provide the presiding judge with written recommendations.

ONE BAD LEMON

Lack Of Communication

Ninety-four-year-old Vera Cordes lay helplessly in her nursing home bed watching a stocky woman dressed in white, a nurse maybe, going through the purse Vera had put on the nightstand.

The room was dark and a sleeping pill had left Vera too drugged to protest, but she knew what she saw at the time. This was in April 1994 and she had just arrived at the Manor Oaks nursing home in northeast Fort Lauderdale after a lengthy hospital stay for a broken hip.

The next morning Vera checked her purse, didn't notice anything missing and chalked it up to the medication and her imagination.

Months later, Vera finally returned home to discover that several of her bank checks had been stolen at some point – and cashed for a total of more than $700 by someone named "Gwenda Lemon." Another $5,000 also had been charged on one of Vera's credit cards to pay for things she knew nothing about.

She reported the incident to the nursing home management and they, in turn, did their own investigation to find that Gwenda Lemon was a former employee who had quit in May. The managers filed a police report with the Fort Lauderdale Police Department.

But it was never assigned to a detective for a follow-up investigation.

In October 1994, a 72-year-old man who was paralyzed from the waist down checked into the Vencor Hospital in downtown Fort Lauderdale. His name was Roy Wilson and he was scheduled for a lengthy hospital stay. While being admitted, he handed his wallet, checkbook and other valuables to the admissions secretary to be put in a safe. She was a pleasant, stocky woman, a new employee.

Roy returned home in late November and, like Vera, went through his bank statements. He found that, while he was in the hospital, a woman called Gwenda Lemon had been cashing his checks. He hadn't realized that they were missing from his checkbook. He was devastated because she cashed 15 of them for more than $17,000.

But he had no idea that Lemon was also the secretary who had taken his property at the hospital. Had he known, he would have alerted the hospital administration. Instead, Roy reported the crime to police in

Pompano Beach, the city where he resided. A patrolman took the
report and filed it as a routine check fraud incident and then, of course,
the paperwork soon was lost among a dozen other cases sitting on an
overworked detective's desk. Crimes against persons, things like rape
and robbery and homicide, understandably receive priority over check
fraud.

Over the next several months, Roy lived each day confined to a
wheelchair in his home, a difficult but routine existence for an elderly
man. But the routine ended in March when a stranger knocked on his
door. Roy opened it up to see a stocky woman dressed in a white nurse's
uniform – a wolf dressed in sheep's clothing.

The woman said that she was a social worker sent by Vencor
Hospital to make sure that his recovery was going well. Roy felt uneasy
because her visit was unexpected, so he asked for identification. She
gave him her driver's license and the infirm old man recognized her
name immediately.

"You're Gwenda Lemon? You stole my checks! You ripped me
off!"

He didn't have a chance to say anymore.

Lemon snatched her driver's license out of his hand, spun him
around in the wheelchair and pushed him through the doorway into his
kitchen. Then she pulled out a can of mace and sprayed his face while
spinning the wheelchair around and around.

The mace brought him instant pain and Roy screamed as it burned
his eyes, nose and skin. His chest tightened up in a reflexive action as he
gasped for air.

He begged her to stop, but she wasn't through yet.

She reached down, firmly grabbed the bottom of the wheelchair and flipped Roy over, head first, onto the kitchen floor, and let his wheelchair land on top of him. Then Lemon maced him again.

He lay whimpering as she ripped the phone out of the wall and walked out of the kitchen, leaving Roy panicked and disoriented on the floor.

He later said that he had waited motionless, fearing another attack, wondering if she would kill him in the end. He could hear her going through paperwork in his office, but he didn't care. Roy listened intently as she walked back towards the kitchen and braced himself for another attack, but it never came. Lemon had found what she wanted and left.

Despite the mauling and his disabilities, Roy managed to crawl to another phone in the house and call police. They arrived in moments and rushed him to the hospital. He would be okay physically, but never the same mentally – always afraid in his own home.

A home invasion robbery report was made and a Pompano Beach detective got on the case immediately. Because Lemon had taken back her driver's license, Roy would have to pick her out of a photo line-up. Then the detective could get an arrest warrant and hunt her down.

The following day, the detective showed Roy the photos of Lemon and five other women who looked similar to her. But there was a problem because the other women were *too* similar in appearance. Roy picked the wrong photograph.

Afterwards, he complained that three of the women could have been the same person, but it was too late. Lemon's photo could not be presented to him legitimately again in another line-up.

Lemon had not eased up at all since her vicious attack against Roy.

She had stolen another seven checks from him that day. Within a week, she had used them to make payments toward her car loan, electric and other bills.

A Pompano Beach detective soon called and asked Lemon in for an interview. She agreed, but also stopped by a furniture rental store on the way to the police station. She still felt brazen enough to use one of Roy's checks to make a payment on her account there.

The detective had hoped to squeeze a confession out of this very bad Lemon. He would need it. The prosecutor had already refused to file charges after Roy's bad identification.

Sadly, Lemon gave the investigator nothing to hang her with.

Despite the detective's efforts to convince her that she would only be admitting the obvious, she looked him in the eye and insisted that she didn't do it, that someone had been impersonating her.

She walked out of the police station a free woman. The detective soon shifted his attention to other cases, those involving rapes and robberies and homicides. Lemon just moved on to new victims.

Four months passed and, in the first week of August 1995, Hurricane Erin bore down on the southeast coast of Florida. The National Hurricane Center issued warnings, which resulted in a mandatory evacuation for the coastal areas of Fort Lauderdale.

A coastal resident named Mary who was in her 70s, checked herself into Vencor Hospital to avoid going to a local hurricane shelter. She never left.

During the elderly woman's hospital stay, Lemon stole and cashed several of Mary's checks for a total of $1,300. Mary became ill unexpectedly, though, and died before police could interview her. Although the death suspiciously coincided with her exploitation by Lemon, hospital medical records cited death by natural causes.

A week later, a 69-year-old woman suffering cancer checked into the same hospital. She would later testify that, when admitted for treatment, she had given her checkbook, food stamps, credit card and cash to the secretary in admissions for "safekeeping." They had disappeared, of course. Lemon had stolen a total of $800 from this frail cancer patient.

Police reports were made for both victims, but the incidents were assigned as fraud investigations to two other detectives who handled such cases. I didn't know about either one at the time.

Throughout this entire period, neither me nor any other cop knew that Lemon was listed as a suspect in multiple elderly exploitation cases in different local police jurisdictions and even within the same agency. She could be described as a "serial exploiter"- someone who exploits a number of elderly victims over time using the same method.

Lemon was a bold, shameless predator with an "in-your-face" approach that effectively victimized many helpless seniors. Unfortunately, a lack of communication between agencies enabled her to continue to prey on the elderly throughout Broward County.

Finally, however, Manor Oaks nursing home contacted me after managers there heard that Lemon was working at Vencor Hospital. They assumed that she already had been arrested for targeting Vera Cordis a full year earlier and wondered how she could still be working in the health care field.

As a result, I ran Lemon's name in the FLPD computer and was shocked to find that she had several complaints against her from the nursing home and hospital. The hospital also advised me that a Pompano Beach detective had been asking about her months earlier. After contacting that detective, I was "off to the races," so to speak.

I focused on obtaining positive identifications and statements from all the victims and, in two weeks time, I had an arrest warrant for Lemon on numerous counts of exploitation and check fraud. But I was disappointed that she wasn't being charged with the home invasion of Roy Wilson. Roy couldn't identify her and she naturally denied committing the crime.

Lemon had quit her job at Vencor Hospital by this time and so, while hunting her down, I tried to figure out a way to get her to admit the home invasion. This had to be done without scaring her into refusing to speak with me at all.

I came up with an idea and finally located her. She was, of all things, a patient in another hospital. Lemon was having a baby. The delivery went fine, but she had a slight fever afterwards and the doctor decided to keep her in the hospital for observation for a couple days.

Before I went into her room to interview Lemon, I spoke with the medical staff and verified that she was not under the influence of any medication that would affect her judgment. Then I walked in, introduced myself and advised her of the arrest warrant.

I assured her that she would not be taken into custody until she was out of the hospital and recovered. Lemon was calm and told me she had known that the police would be coming for her eventually. She was actually grateful for the delay in the arrest and agreeable to discussing the charges.

I decided that it was time to make my move.

"Gwenda, you seem like a decent person to me, but the prosecutor doesn't agree. He's the one who decides to charge, or not charge, you for the home invasion robbery of Roy Wilson. That's the charge that you really have to worry about."

She watched me intently and remained silent. And now the lies...

"I already have proof that you were there that evening. I had the wheelchair processed for fingerprints and yours were lifted from the bottom of it. What bothers me, though, is that Mr. Wilson has several prior complaints against him by prostitutes. It appears that he invites them into his home and then tries to assault them."

She smiled a little and started shaking her head up and down. Bingo!

"Yes, I was there, but he attacked me. He would give me money to show him my titties, but then he wanted to touch them and I wouldn't let him. He offered me more money and I said no, because I don't go that far. I'm not that kind of person. Then he became angry and pulled out some mace and started spraying me all over!"

"A pervert, eh? So what did you do, spray him back?"

"No, I didn't. I just held up the couch pillows to try to block it and ran out of the house. I never sprayed him, I swear it."

The lies worked.

Roy had no prior police complaints involving prostitution or anything else and Lemon's fingerprints were never lifted from his wheelchair. I just had needed her to admit being there and now she had. And not only that. Lemon actually had given me a statement *insisting* that she was there.

The prosecutor was delighted and filed additional charges of burglary of an occupied dwelling and battery on an elderly person, two serious felonies.

I arrested Lemon on February 7, 1996. It was a "no bond" arrest, which meant that she should have been held in jail right through her trial dates.

But my cases just don't end that easily.

Lemon's attorney was granted a bond hearing and the presiding judge was the same woman that I had written about in an earlier chapter, Judge Susan "Let' em Go" Lebow.

The hearing proceeded as bond hearings normally do. The prosecutor argued that the defendant should stay in jail because she was a flight risk and a danger to the community. The defense argued that I had tricked Lemon into giving me a statement and that she was actually an upstanding, peaceful citizen with a new baby.

Judge Lebow listened to both sides and ruled that my tactic of tricking Lemon into incriminating herself did not violate any constitutional rights, but she also ruled in favor of granting bond. Lemon bonded out the same week of her arrest. She was a free woman again and this time managed to avoid assaulting others.

At least, for several months.

On July 13, 1996, Lemon climbed into her car armed with a handgun and drove to a house in the tough northwest section of Fort Lauderdale. Her husband had been shot and wounded that morning during a dispute there. Lemon believed that the shooter was inside the home and she wanted revenge.

On arriving, she scrambled out of the car and fired several shots through the front picture window. Witnesses watched her throwing a tantrum and shouting obscenities on the front lawn before finally driving away. Two adults and several children were in the house at the time. Fortunately, they were not injured.

Lemon also didn't show up for her scheduled court appearances and Judge Lebow finally issued a bench warrant for her arrest. This dangerous criminal was taken into custody in her home and that arrest stuck.

Lemon remained in jail until June 1997, when she plead guilty to a dozen felony charges. Judge Lebow had had enough and sentenced her to eight years in prison. Justice was finally served.

A year earlier, Vera Cordes was quoted on Lemon in the papers as saying, "She had a good time, didn't she? The fact that she was out there doing it to other people, that's what bothered me."

But Vera died before Lemon's final arrest. In fact, half of Lemon's elderly victims were deceased by the time that she was sentenced.

CHAPTER 10

PERSPECTIVE & PREVENTION
Myths

When reading an article about elderly abuse in the New York Times I noticed that the author began by describing it as, "…the neglected stepchild of domestic violence and child abuse in the triangle of human violence."

I was puzzled because I've never looked at elderly abuse as an "offspring" of anything, but the article still offered an interesting account of two elderly sisters in Brooklyn who lost their home and life savings to support their nephew's crack habit.

The nephew had abused them physically and mentally when they wouldn't give him money. After they finally gave everything they had to him, he sent them out on the street to beg strangers for more.

A picture of the two victims walking down a Brooklyn sidewalk as bag ladies capped the article and effectively gave the reader reason to be angry.

What also caught my attention, though, was that the author went on to describe elderly abuse as "one of the more brutal yet poorly understood plagues."

The "plague" part may have been stretching things, but the "brutal and poorly understood" part was right on the mark. Exploitation is prevalent because it is misunderstood and here are three of the most common misunderstandings, or "myths."

"Exploiters typically have criminal records."

False. The majority of suspects that I have investigated did not have criminal records. Many had reputable backgrounds. However, most had financial troubles and few assets.

"The greater a person's income level, the greater their risk of being exploited."

Statistically, no one socioeconomic group is targeted more than another.

"Elderly persons with mental disabilities process information slower but offset these infirmities with experience and wisdom."

Elderly persons who suffer acute short-term memory loss or other mental infirmities no longer have the ability to understand financial issues and they lack the capacity to give consent regarding financial matters. This has nothing to do with experience or wisdom.

So an exploiter is not always going to be a prior convicted felon and the victim does not have to be wealthy and naïve.

Exploitation Vs. Fraud

A person can obtain a better perspective of this crime by looking at the correct definitions of fraud and exploitation taken from state law and the dictionary. As stated in the introduction, fraud is essentially based on deception; the false and deceptive statement of fact intended to induce another person to give up a valuable item he or she owns. Normally scams and confidence games intended to entice a competent victim are placed in this category. "Choice" is involved and most state laws are written with the assumption that fraud victims have the capacity to weigh information and make decisions based on that information.

But when the victim doesn't have the capacity to make financial decisions and the culprit takes advantage of this disability, this in fact is an exploitation crime. The dictionary defines exploitation as "the using or taking advantage of someone in an organized or systematic way." Deception is not mentioned.

Florida state law defines an exploitation victim as "a person 60 years of age or older who is suffering from the infirmities of aging as manifested by advanced age or organic brain damage, or other physical, mental, or emotional dysfunctioning, to the extent that the ability of the person to provide adequately for the person's own care or protection is impaired."

An exploitation crime occurs when someone takes advantage of the vulnerability or dependant condition of a disabled elderly person to deprive that person of their assets. Although deceptive tactics like false statements or promises are often used during an exploitation crime they are not always necessary because the victim is disabled. This is why deception is not the primary issue to this crime.

For example, if a landscaper knocked on your door and offered to mow your lawn for $1,500 you would probably laugh in his face and slam the door. Even if you chose to pay him that absurd amount a crime was not committed because he was upfront with the price beforehand and did not use deception.

But if a landscaper who normally charges $25 to mow a lawn sees that an elderly woman is clearly confused and takes advantage of her by charging $1500, this is exploitation of the elderly. He was upfront about the price but took advantage of the fact that she couldn't tell the difference between $25 and $1,500. He didn't deceive her with false statements or promises because he didn't have to. He was exploiting her disability.

Public Perception

Because exploitation is misunderstood, those who witness it either do the wrong thing or nothing at all to prevent it. Witnesses often fail to act because they mistakenly believe that confused victims don't have capacity but must be treated as if they did. I can recall countless occasions when bank tellers knowingly allowed victims without capacity to withdraw thousands of dollars from their accounts while suspects stood beside them at teller windows. The tellers later testified that they thought they had to comply with the confused victim's request.

Attorneys have been known to shy away from pursuing criminal investigations on behalf of their clients because they couldn't justify charging the mentally infirm victims exorbitant fees. How would an attorney claim that an elderly person chose to retain his or her services at a specified rate per hour and insist with the same breath that the client doesn't have the capacity to make financial decisions?

Government Perception

Many government and private agencies often provide the wrong advice to the public on how to recognize and deal with exploitation because they conflate the crime with fraud crimes that are normally committed against victims who have capacity. For example, advice on how to prevent identity theft or telemarketing fraud is intended for those who are still able to make financial decisions. But when exploitation is incorporated into fraud, fraud-prevention advice tends to be the norm for both crimes. For example, to be wary of sweepstakes telemarketers is good fraud prevention advice, but how could you expect a person without capacity to understand and retain this information? Elderly people who are legally blind must often trust caretakers or others outside their family with personal information, financial transactions and intimate details of their lives. It offers them no help when a government agency prints pamphlets saying, "Never give out personal information to someone that you don't know." Although fraud prevention tips make good advice for seniors who are not impaired, it should not be considered a deterrent to exploitation crimes.

Training provided by many law enforcement agencies to police has historically been inadequate and I myself was guilty of misinterpreting what was probably an exploitation crime in progress due to lack of training. While assigned to patrol many years ago, I became involved in a car chase through the streets of Fort Lauderdale following a vehicle that was traveling erratically on a flat tire. Sparks were flying everywhere as the car weaved in and out of traffic in what appeared to be more of a chase in slow motion than "high-speed." When it ended, I extracted three drunken youths from the vehicle but a fourth person, a 91-year-old man, was found sitting silently in the back seat with a timid smile on his face. I mistook his vague answers to my simple questions as a feeble attempt to be evasive and considered him "foolish", so I arrested him along with the others. I realize now that those youths were probably taking advantage of him. If I had been trained properly, I would have protected rather than punished this man for being disabled.

Why The Government Can't Always Help

Each state has a social service agency that responds to elderly abuse complaints and the agencies are commonly titled, "Adult Protective Services" (APS). These agencies provide both investigative and support services to elderly and disabled victims of abuse, neglect and exploitation. But these are civil agencies without arrest powers. Laws exist that require APS agencies to work jointly and cooperatively with there local police agencies during these investigations. The responsibility to lock up exploitation culprits lies with local, state and federal law enforcement agencies. But three things hinder appropriate police response: training, resources and inherent evidentiary weaknesses that arise during criminal investigations.

As stated, special training on how the police can recognize exploitation and interact with elderly victims is often insufficient. Yet even a trained and timely response can still be hindered by inherent investigative pitfalls. The elderly are referred to as "silent victims," not only because their victimization goes unreported, but also because they are unable or unwilling to provide witness to the crime to complete a criminal investigation.

States have many regulatory and criminal laws that are designed to protect the elderly population. For example, Florida law makes it a felony to abuse, neglect, or exploit an elderly or disabled person; a special law automatically upgrades the criminal penalty for anyone who commits battery on a person 65-years of age or older. Besides mandatory reporting laws, there are state agencies that license, regulate and enforce all the professions that provide services to the elderly.

Victim Characteristics

There are two common types. The first suffer mental infirmities.

Exploitation victims who suffer short-term memory loss or other mental infirmities, and therefore lack the capacity to give consent, often live alone. They normally appear timid, trusting, anxious and are almost always unaware that they have been victimized. They often become embarrassed when confronted with the issue of their memory loss and try to hide it with excuses and rationalizations. When told they have been cheated, they do not want to prosecute and often feel as if they have done something wrong.

These are the perfect victims and the easiest to exploit. Even if their victimization somehow is reported to authorities, they will not complain should their case fall through the legal cracks. They're not capable of understanding so they cannot complain.

Victims who have mental capacity but suffer physical disabilities can be quite different. They know that their trust was violated. They desire prosecution, sometimes passionately, and make good witnesses. They often show resolve to see the matter through the legal system. Ironically, the biggest stumbling block to this can be their infirmities. As we've seen with some cases described in this book, these victims sometimes don't live long enough for their cases to reach the courts.

Suspect Characteristics

Exploiters can be those who provide services to the elderly or not. Exploiters can be professionals who make a living out of it or they may be opportunists. They may know their victims intimately or may be complete strangers. They may be caretakers, financial advisors, or simply those who have access to an infirm elderly person and his/her assets. They could be family members or neighbors. I have investigated religious leaders, fellow police officers, guardians, geriatric case managers, and even other senior citizens for the crime of exploiting the elderly. They can often appear to be upstanding citizens. Remember the friendly tenants, health care worker and priest in earlier chapters.

The most common type of culprit is the "altruistic exploiter," a rationalizer and manipulator who plays the part of a do-gooder throughout the commission of the crime. Their most obvious trait is that they keep taking and taking, though claiming to be giving, loving and sacrificing for the victim. They usually step into the victim's life in some type of a caretaker role. They contradict themselves by claiming that the victim is competent when he/she is clearly not, but insisting that the victim is "confused" when the victim is the accuser. They insist that the victim's assets were "gifts," loans, or payment for services rendered. They isolate the victim while claiming that they are protecting him or her.

Watch for signs of abuse or neglect by the suspect because exploitation is often the motive for both.

The second type of culprit is the "opportunistic exploiter." They are normally people who provide some type of service to the public and simply take advantage of opportunities when working for a vulnerable senior citizen.

This type of exploiter could be a landscaper who charges $5,000 to mow the lawn because the victim could not differentiate between that amount and $50. Or it could be the plumber who takes $1,250 from an old blind woman to fix her leaky faucet because she trusted him to fill out her check for $125.

The opportunistic exploiter operates under the premise that if the victim doesn't know, then no one else will.

PREVENTION

So what then is good prevention advice to avoid exploitation?

The dynamics of our aging population, specifically the upcoming "boom" of the baby boomers, will allow exploitation to grow out of control unless proper preventative action is taken beforehand. That old saying, "The best offense is a good defense" applies perfectly here. There are relatively easy legal and financial steps to take to prevent someone from emptying your bank accounts or stealing your home after you lose capacity.

One option is to add the name of a trusted person to an elder's bank accounts in an "or" capacity. This would allow either person free access to the accounts, including making withdrawals, without the other's signature or consent. But this would also give the co-signer the freedom to monitor the accounts and the bank would have the freedom to notify this trusted person immediately if they were concerned about suspicious activity. This is a simple and cheap option, but it can also be potentially dangerous. Remember that family members and those close to victims are often the culprits.

To prevent an exploiter from stealing your home through a simple quitclaim deed, you could add the name of a trusted person as co-owner. This additional signature would be required to legally transfer ownership, and if forged, that person could testify as a solid witness in civil and criminal courts against the culprit when you may be unable to. Again, keep in mind that you are giving this trusted person part ownership legally to your property with this option.

Advanced Directives

A recommended and safer option would be referring to an elder law attorney and using advanced directives to protect your assets for the future. Advanced directives are contracts that designate another person to act on your behalf when you are no longer able to. An example would be a living will, which allows you to designate another person to make medical decisions on your behalf when you no longer can. You can hire an elder law attorney to draw up an advanced directive like a trust. Most trusts are called "grantor trusts" and these are contracts between the person setting up the trust and the trustee. If a victim sets up a trust, then after he or she loses capacity, the management of the assets will fall into the hands of whoever is chosen to be the trustee. If a person does not have someone to designate as trustee then a good choice would be a corporate fiduciary, like a trust officer at a bank. Another benefit of a trust is that setting up an estate is often no longer necessary.

Finally, a reasonable and simple advanced directive is called a durable power of attorney. This is a contract that a person can sign that would simply designate a person of choice to make financial decisions on your behalf after your loss of capacity.

Protecting A Disabled Loved One

When an elder shows clear signs of short-term memory loss to the point where they may no longer be able to make financial decisions or care for themselves, bring him or her to their personal physician and ask that he note in the elder's chart any early signs of dementia or mental impairment. This may end up providing crucial expert testimony if the elder is exploited in the future.

When dealing with the elder care industry keep in mind that certain credentials can be misleading. The term "gerontologist" is not defined and regulated by law in all states, and in states like Florida the term "doctor" can be used freely as long as the person does not represent themselves as a medical doctor (M.D.).

A "non-profit organization" is not a charity. It is simply an incorporated organization that presents itself as existing for educational or charitable reasons from which it's shareholders or trustees cannot benefit financially...but the employees can. A non-profit organization can take in $1,000,000 in donations and pay a major portion of that to its employees.

Here are two basic options to pursue to provide oversight and care for a disabled elder:

Guardianship-   A guardian is a court appointed person who makes decisions on behalf of an incapacitated person. Guardianship is designed to protect an elderly person from abuse, neglect and exploitation while preserving that person's rights. A formal guardianship is the safest course to take to protect a disabled elder, but it can be a time-consuming and costly process. Guardianships are not fool-proof and I have arrested guardians on several occasions for exploiting their wards, but this is still generally a good option because of the regulation involved. The guardian's activities are overseen by the courts to ensure that they are not abusing their position.

Geriatric Care Management- Hiring a Geriatric Care Manager, someone paid on an hourly basis to manage finances and arrange proper care for an elder, is a quick and easy process. But there are no regulations, no oversight in place to ensure that the case manager will act honestly and responsibly with the victim's assets. So a trusted person chosen by the elder to oversee the case manager's activities makes sense.

Final Thoughts

Although the cases presented from my files are dated, there is no reason to believe that conditions have really changed over the years. Exploitation crimes still prevail for the same reasons and a better understanding of the crime is needed to combat it.

I wrote this book to give the reader just that, a better understanding to prevent victimization effectively. This final chapter began with a quote from an article where the author referred to elderly abuse in general as

"...the neglected stepchild of domestic violence and child abuse in the triangle of human violence."

Exploitation of the elderly is not just "fraud" nor is it the "neglected stepchild of domestic violence." It is another expression of the misunderstood dark side of human behavior, where one of us takes advantage of another's misfortune for personal gain. It will never be stopped completely, but could most certainly be reduced significantly.

The irony of all of this is that soon today's baby-boomers will become tomorrow's elderly and potentially tomorrow's victims. We're all in the same boat, no matter what our ages.

So it would be fitting to end this book with a quote taken from the 16th century poet, John Donne.

...I am involved in mankind; and therefore never send to know for whom the bell tolls; it tolls for thee.

Donne is saying that whatever affects one of us affects us all. The way that we deal with elderly crimes today reflects on the type of people that we are now and will have a direct bearing on our own personal safety tomorrow.

~ You can contact this author through his "Storefront Page" at www.lulu.com ~